D0426588

Making Change Happen One Person at a Time

Making Change Happen One Person at a Time

Assessing Change Capacity within Your Organization

Charles H. Bishop, Jr.

AMACOM
American Management Association
New York • Atlanta • Boston • Chicago • Kansas City • San Francisco • Washington, D.C.
Brussels • Mexico City • Tokyo • Toronto

This publication is designed to provide accurate and authoritative information in regard to the subject matter covered. It is sold with the
understanding that the publisher is not engaged in rendering legal,
accounting, or other professional service. If legal advice or other expert assistance is required, the services of a competent professional
person should be sought.

Library of Congress Cataloging-in-Publication Data

Bishop, Charles H., Ph.D.
       Making change happen one person at a time: assessing change
   capacity within your organization / Charles H. Bishop.
           p.   cm.
       Includes index.
       ISBN 0-8144-0528-2
       1. Organizational change—Handbooks, manuals, etc.
     2. Interpersonal relations—Handbooks, manuals, etc.   I. Title.

   HD58.8.B527   2000
   658.4'06—dc21

                                                      00-029965

Printing number

10   9   8   7   6   5   4   3   2   1

To my creative, supportive, and caring wife **Paula** and great children, **Mike** and **Amy.** All A-Players in their own right. Just . . . the best!

Contents

Preface
A Process for Making
Change Happen

If you're attempting to drive change—in your team, your department, or your organization—you can do so in many different ways. You can create a brilliant change strategy. You can throw money at the change program. You can inspire and motivate your people to make the required changes. You can use your organization's human resources (HR) programs and tools to develop people in change-friendly ways. But if you lack the right people, your change efforts will be fatally flawed.

Who are the right people? Who is best able to plan, lead, manage, and implement the required changes? This is a matter of some debate. Certain organizations rely on the HR staff for the training and development associated with a change strategy while assigning the "more important" strategic and planning roles to management and functional teams. In some companies, people who are in the top leadership positions are directly and intimately involved. In still others, change-agent and change-leader positions are rewards for "technical" accomplishments—for those who achieve or exceed performance objectives.

The larger issue, however, is whether these people are capable of taking on new and expanded roles and responsibilities in changing environments. Are they A-players who can make change happen when placed in key positions? Are they

B-players who will provide support for a change program and can handle some new challenges but should not be placed in pivotal positions? Are they C-players who are only comfortable with changes within their limited area of expertise? Or are they D-players who will resist change and may even sabotage a change program?[1] These are complex assessments. You can't tell if people are A-, B-, C-, or D-players just by examining their performance review, job history, and skill sets. It all depends on each individual's "personal change capacity," and it's doubtful if you have a reading on that capacity, even if you are an HR person accustomed to making performance assessments. That's scary, especially for senior managers, since they honestly don't know if they possess the talent necessary to achieve their strategic objectives.

Later in this preface, I'll give you a better sense of who these A-, B-, C-, and D-players are, based on their personal change capacity. For now, let's look at this issue through the lens of a simple scenario:

> Imagine you've been chosen to plan and implement a crucial change strategy for your organization. To make this change happen, you need to choose exactly the right people for ten change leadership positions. Your margin for error is 10 percent; you're allowed to mismatch one person with one position. Any more mistakes and the change effort will fail. Your job is on the line. In fact, your boss has told you that if this change strategy isn't effective, the company will be in trouble and jobs will be in jeopardy. Given this responsibility, there's one question you need to answer: How confident do you feel about choosing the right people for the right positions?

Without a proven process and tools, it's difficult to be confident. This book is written to provide you with this process and tools. By using it, you'll avoid the following mistakes:

▲ Placing someone in a key change position based solely on competencies or a performance-rating scheme

▲ Overlooking a critical development need that can hamper an individual's ability to cope with a change-based role

▲ Putting a potential A-player in a change role that fails to capitalize on the individual's towering strengths (and that brings out weaknesses)

▲ Failing to use HR people and processes in ways that enhance change capacity

▲ Believing a C-player will automatically respond well to a change initiative, continuing to be the same solid performer in a changing environment when asked to take on new and expanded roles and responsibilities

Why It's Easy to Put the Wrong Person in the Right Job

Let's look at an example of the last mistake—believing a C-player will automatically respond well to a change initiative—in order to understand how critical it is to assess personal change capacity accurately. Jack is a solid sales manager with a large corporation, and he's consistently helped his group meet its quotas and has established strong and long relationships with customers. As part of an overall change program mandated by a new CEO, Jack was chosen to help transform the strategy and operating systems of the sales group. Unfortunately, he was the wrong choice to fulfill the CEO's promise to the shareholders that "we are committed to reworking how we go to market."

Jack was chosen to be part of the change program because, in his boss's words, "He is one of our best." There's no question that Jack was a solid producer as a salesperson for seven years and that he made a good transition to sales manager three years ago. Plus, Jack's highly confident, aggressive, and not afraid to take a risk, qualities that Jack's boss felt would serve the company well as it reworked the sales group's strategy and systems. In addition, Jack's boss recognized that Jack needed to grow as a manager and leader, and he was convinced that this was the perfect opportunity to facilitate that growth.

So Jack was thrust into his new role and failed miserably. He was not strategically agile, his ideas were nothing more than recycled versions of previous tactical plans, and he was contentious and had trouble working with peers.

All of this could have been anticipated if a serious assessment had been conducted. Jack might have made a significant contribution to the change effort in the right role and with the right development plan, but without an assessment this wasn't possible. Jack's boss made assumptions about his personal change capacity that were erroneous. If questions were asked and issues probed, his boss would have discovered that the former senior vice president of sales had been frustrated with Jack's stubbornness and lack of original ideas on an important project two years ago. He would have heard stories about how Jack tends to dig into a position and refuse to adapt to new circumstances.

The ramifications of Jack's failure are far-reaching. It's not only Jack's career within the organization that suffers, but Jack's boss takes a great deal of heat for his recommendation that Jack be part of the change team. When the company is unable to change its sales strategy and operating system in ways that improve productivity or service support, the CEO is reprimanded by the board of directors and this misstep is one of the factors that leads to his resignation.

No one knew it to look at him, but Jack was a C-player. Organizations are filled with C-players like Jack, people who do their jobs competently and are looked upon favorably by their bosses, but fail to respond to the challenge of change. There's a disturbing lack of assessment in the selection of people who participate in the change process. By dumb luck, sometimes individuals capable of responding positively are picked to lead and manage change, but this capability rarely becomes reality. They can't perform effectively because there's a mismatch between who they are and what their change role requires. Managers and HR people therefore need to share a process that assesses for change capacity and not just performance.

How This Process Evolved

Making the right match is what I've helped some of the world's best companies accomplish. Let me give you a brief history of how I created the process and tools that make this possible.

As a senior associate with Kepner-Tregoe consulting firm in the 1970s, I worked on many projects designed to improve organizations and executive decision making. It was here that I began working on a process for finding the talent necessary to achieve organizational strategies. When I joined Federal Express in the late 1970s, I had the chance to test and refine this process. As an HR executive, I was given responsibility for revamping the selection process to deal with the company's explosive growth. Fred Smith, the company's president and CEO, was pushing his theme of "people, service, and profitability," with an emphasis on finding the right people for the pivotal positions of "city managers"—the people supervising Federal Express's move to grow its distribution channels.

While elements of the personal change capacity tools you'll find in this book were developed at Federal Express, the model really started to take shape at Baxter International in the 1980s. As the vice president for leadership development, I helped put a system in place to help evaluate talent for the new key positions created in a scaled-down company, the result of healthcare deregulation. Using research pioneered at the Center for Creative Leadership as well as other resources, we formulated a "human asset inventory" that became a crucial tool for Baxter to evaluate talent and then place and develop individuals for important change-related positions.

At NationsBank, I discovered that the human asset inventory could be used to assess talent to achieve a completely different strategic objective. We needed to assimilate new bank acquisitions into the system, which meant that a significant number of people had to be evaluated quickly and perceptively to ensure a smooth transition. We discovered that our tool was astonishingly effective at spotlighting the strengths and weaknesses of key people relative to the objectives for the acquired companies; we were able to identify who was going to add value within the context of the acquisition strategy and who was likely to destroy it.

At Quaker Oats and ADT Security Services, I continued to assess the personal change capacity of a wide variety of people relative to each company's change strategy. At ADT, where I was senior vice president of HR, it was especially effective and was viewed as one of the catalysts for driving the business in new, more productive directions; the stock price appreciated over 100 percent in fifteen months. To prepare to make significant changes to our service delivery training, benefits and compensation, and other systems, we couldn't afford to have people in place who resisted change or failed to lead it with vision and innovation. In evaluating talent, we discovered that some of the people with high personal change capacities had been buried and weren't being considered for key positions while others who were being considered were change resistant in a variety of ways. By getting the right people in the right positions, we made a significant contribution to the change effort.

Even more significantly, we established a clear linkage between people and profitability in changing environments. At each organization, two compelling themes emerged with hindsight:

1. When change failed and profits fell, it was because we tolerated people in key positions who weren't A-players, who lacked the versatility and responsiveness to change that was required.

2. When change succeeded and profits rose, it was because we made sure we had A-players in key positions, moving B-, C-, and D-players out of these positions no matter how much seniority or clout they possessed. Time after time, we found that placing the right people in the right positions during periods of change translated into reduced costs, smart investments, breakthrough products, and so on. The right people didn't just make change happen; they made it happen profitably. More than anything else, this observation convinced me that my methodology would benefit others.

Throughout this book, I'll refer to my experiences at these organizations as well as to my consulting work with a variety of other companies. At times, I'll refer to organizations by name. In other instances (especially when organizations blundered and failed to consider the personal change capacity of their people), I won't name names.

A Process Rooted in Individual Assessments

To bring about effective change, you must help your group or organization through the following process:

1. Assess the personal change capacity of your key people.
2. Create development plans in line with personal change capacity assessments.
3. Determine organizational change capacity and its impact on personal change capacity.

The most challenging and important task, however, is the first one. If you incorrectly assess the personal change capacity of key people, you'll taint the rest of the process. While the book will help you with all three requirements, its initial focus will be on getting the first one right. To that end, let's define the four individual assessment categories that you need to know.

A-Players

These people not only respond positively to change but they drive it. They may be relative newcomers to organizations or veterans, junior or top executives, but what unites them is the way in which they greet change as a friend rather than an enemy. When they learn about a new program or strategy, they're eager to experience a new way of doing things and often volunteer ideas to facilitate and drive a new approach. They are not naive about what's required to accomplish a new task, and they are more than willing to push back against an assignment and help shape the effort.

Invariably, teams with A-players work better and embrace problematic issues as challenges; they make the people around them more effective. They also produce results, no matter what the assignment is. If they're in research and development, they find a way to reduce product development cycle time. If they're in finance, they come up with an innovative method to reduce the budget. And they do these things consistently.

Sue is the quintessential A-player. An HR professional with a midsize communications company, Sue had been with her company for three years when it was purchased by a foreign communication conglomerate. As rumors of downsizing and other changes swirled, some of Sue's colleagues tried to be inconspicuous while others focused on making their performance look good on paper. Sue saw the acquisition as a tremendous opportunity. Dissatisfied with the conservative, status quo mind-set of the company, Sue drew up a plan to restructure a segment of the HR department in response to a request from a "relationship manager" employed by the acquiring company. Sue was taking a risk with her restructuring idea; she had no way of knowing if it would rub the relationship manager the wrong way. But she was eager to try her idea out on a fresh set of ears after trying and failing to convince her boss that this was an important step for the company. Not only was her idea enthusiastically received by the relationship manager, but Sue was eventually put in charge of a restructuring program that affected the entire HR function.

B-Players

This label describes individuals who are generally receptive to change but lack the perspective, enthusiasm, and change leadership abilities of A-players or are only willing to embrace certain types of change. Although B-players can contribute significantly to change efforts, they may need a significant amount of development before they can assume pivotal roles. B-players often have excellent performance records and hold key jobs in the organization, but they only perform well if the conditions are right. If a major change occurs and they're asked to drive a restructuring or to play a major role in a global marketing initiative, they may not respond with energy or initiative.

As a vice president of operations, Harold has risen quickly through his Fortune 500 company. He went to Harvard Business School, performed well for one of the world's largest packaged-goods companies, and arrived at this present employer as a middle manager. Harold has been instrumental in streamlining a number of the company's processes, saving them money, and increasing productivity in the process. While he has demonstrated a solid response to change in these situations, he's also been gun-shy about change when non-process issues were involved. For instance, Harold has subtly but consistently resisted the new CEO's insistence that more work be done in teams. Although Harold has set up some teams, he hasn't provided them with the resources or leadership necessary for them to do their work with optimum effectiveness.

C-Players

In a sense, these are the silent majority in many organizations. Frequently technically proficient, the C-player's competence often gets confused with change responsiveness. While C-players may be willing to try new methods and approaches in technical areas with which they're familiar, other types of change give them cold feet. The assumption, however, is that "they'll adjust" to new approaches outside of their areas of competence. Their bosses assume that these people just need some time to orient themselves to a new process, or they need more information before they embrace a new strategy. Sometimes C-players occupy key positions in an organization, and management is counting on them to lead the implementation of a new strategy. Not only is a great deal of development needed before they exhibit such leadership, but it's possible that they're only capable of being support players in a changing environment. Many C-players aren't sufficiently adaptable and flexible to become change agents and may even resist taking on any new roles or responsibilities. At best, their history of responding positively to change is spotty.

Jack, described earlier, is a typical example of a C-player.

D-Players

They're change resisters of the first rank. They consistently exhibit an antipathy toward every new program announced by management. Like C-players, they may be technically competent. But even in these areas, they are rigid and conservative. Innovation, risk taking, and anything else that requires a fresh perspective rub them the wrong way. Their resistance to change may be active as well as passive. They may sabotage a new process or policy through their actions or in their conversations with peers and direct reports.

Margie is a D-player who is a brand manager for a large consumer-electronics company. Her brand is well-known and has earned a good deal of equity over the years. While most of the brand's products aren't market leaders, they've performed relatively well until recently. Strong competition from abroad, however, has seriously hurt several of the brands, and a new marketing vice president has the CEO's support in pursuing aggressive new advertising and promotion strategies. While Margie pretends to be following her new marketing V.P.'s lead, she's dragging her feet. Margie has stretched out the search for a new advertising agency to almost a year, and she's made only superficial changes to her strategy for the brand in the coming years—superficial changes that may fool her boss into thinking that she's buying into the new marketing initiative.

How Well Do You Know Your ABC's and D's?

The most effective twenty-first-century managers and HR departments will be able to categorize the personal change capability of people based on these letter grades and develop them accordingly. If you can make an accurate assessment, you can accelerate the pace of change and enhance the effectiveness of any change strategy. Whether you're a manager making incremental policy changes, an HR director attempting to support your company's change efforts,[2] or a CEO attempting to transform the organization, you will benefit from personal change capacity information. Imagine being able to place exactly the right people in key change-management positions; or being able to provide hiring, selection, and training recommendations keyed to personal change capacity; or having the ability to anticipate development needs that will help employees double their effectiveness in a change-based environment; or knowing which people are most likely to resist or even sabotage a change effort.

Before introducing you to the process that will make all this possible, I'd like you to think about how prepared you are to analyze the change capacity of the people who work with you. The following exercise is designed to assess your preparedness.

Assessment Quotient

Write down the name of any direct report who has worked with you for at least a year and who has performed competently. Then answer the following questions about that individual:

1. Is this individual a sponge for new knowledge and skills; would she willingly spend significant time and energy to acquire this knowledge and skills?

2. Is the direct report the sort of person who inspires others to learn; is he capable of motivating other people to make sacrifices in order to learn new ways of working?

3. Is she able to adapt easily to complexity, ambiguity, paradox, and uncertainty?

4. Will he adapt well to an expanded role that calls on him to lead, manage, or work in ways that are unfamiliar to him, or that requires him to change beliefs and behaviors he's held for a long time?

5. If a change program called for the individual to work longer and harder than ever before, would she resist it?

6. If a change program called for him to work with people, processes, or policies that were very different from those he had known, would he resist it?

7. If you gave this person a difficult but important role in a changed company (or team or department), are you certain she wouldn't react by following a well-known script (versus responding to the unique needs of the situation)?

8. Let's say a change effort calls for someone to have significant expertise or ability in a given area. Do you know this person well enough to determine whether he possesses this tremendous expertise?

9. Do you know what development plan you might create to turn this person from a borderline performer in a changed environment into a solid contributor? If so, is there sufficient time for this person to develop, given the organizational need?

10. You're asked by your boss if this person should be given an expanded leadership role in the change effort, placed in a support position, or kept out of the process entirely. Do you feel certain you know the right answer?

11. Would you characterize this individual as an A-, B-, C-, or D-player?

If you are like most people, you can only answer a few of these questions with any degree of certainty. If you've worked with people for years and they've never been asked to make major changes, it's very difficult to know how they'll react. Or they may have seemed to respond positively to a change program in the past, but in reality they only gave lip service to the new process, complaining bitterly to fellow workers about what they were being asked to do. As a manager or even as a highly perceptive (about people) HR specialist, you're likely to be reduced to guessing about the change capacity of key people. Or even worse, you're likely to overestimate their change capacity because they performed well in low-change environments and you expect their performance to carry over to high-change situations.

Most managers haven't been trained and lack experience in assessing personal change capacity. While most managers know their people's skills and weaknesses, they don't know how to evaluate an individual's response to change in the past, ability to take on new and larger roles in the future, and the other factors that determine if someone is an A-, B-, C-, or D-player. Certainly, some HR people are also psychologists and have been trained to identify traits that might make people resistant to change. I've found, however, that psychological skills and instruments are relatively useless when it comes to identifying change capacity. There are simply too many work-context issues involved to make a purely psychological approach effective.

All this presents significant challenges for managers and HR folks, yet they are the ones that the process, presented in the Introduction, will greatly facilitate.

Acknowledgments

From an editorial standpoint: Adrienne Hickey, for making a leap of faith in this area of change and her willingness to invest time and counsel to bring this book forward. Bruce Wexler . . . I could not have written this book without his clarity of thinking and willingness to challenge and keep me focused, his wisdom and common sense, his ability to shape and distill common sense out of my concepts—a trusted ally.

The stimulation that contributed to ideas in this book came from many sources and in a variety of forms. The following CEOs were major contributors to these concepts and beliefs in those early formative times:

▲ Fred Smith, Art Bass, Frank Maguire, and Jim Barksdale at Federal Express
▲ Rick Adam at Baxter International
▲ Harold Chandler and Pat Flinn at NationsBank

All of these senior leaders of change continually forced the issue of people and human resources (HR) into the mainstream of the business. For that lesson and discipline I will be eternally grateful.

Many of my HR colleagues and consultants in this journey, including Tony Rucci, Jim Karis, Jim Shanley, John Harris, Geary Rummler, David Morrison, Pat Dailey, Bob Miles, Bill Jensen, Jim Peters, Bill Bowen, Bruce Saari, and Jack Berry—all outstanding talent—challenged and added much to my understanding and convictions. Tony Rucci was the individual who made me aware of the power of Team Assessments of talent and probably should get an extra thanks.

Nonprofit organizations such as the Center for Creative Leadership (CCL) and research by Morgan McCall, Kerry Bunker, and Mike Lombardo were significant inflection points in my personal development and my application of the ideas inside organizations. The Human Resources Planning Society has played a major role in platforming and testing some of these concepts. Most recently, the excellent studies by the Corporate Leadership Council have advanced the ideas in this field. Most notable is the series about the future of HR.

As a practitioner, Bob Eichenger in his early work at Pepsico brought many of the ideas from CCL to fruition. Mike Lombardo and Eichenger formed Lominger, which continues to make significant contributions to the issue of development of talent and the overall profession. Jim Shanley at Bank of America continues to push the envelope.

Organizations that have done these things "right"— companies such as General Electric, Pepsico, and NationsBank —contributed much to the ideas. Quite frankly, sharing ideas back and forth with my colleagues inside those organizations makes it difficult to know with absolute certainty the origin of some of the concepts. For example, when working with Jim Shanley and Pat Dailey you always knew that your product would be better because of the collaboration.

Organizations making progress in this "people area" are fun to be involved with and they will, in the near future, be as well-known as some other organizations. They include Sunbeam, in its turnaround under Jerry Levin with Ron Dunbar and Gary Chant; First Data Corporation, with Myron Beard and Marylou Straub . . . they are doing the right things. Lucent Technologies, under Pat Dailey, and Bank of America, with Jim Shanley, just keep getting better and better.

The experience at Quaker Oats (in the early to mid-1990s) had its own unique "lessons learned." During that time I saw many A-players who were attempting to make change and they contributed to the ideas contained herein. A-players such as Phil Marineau (now CEO of Levi-Strauss), Jim Doyle (president of Gatorade), Chuck Marcy (now CEO of Horizon Organic

Dairy), and Mike Zawalski (now president of Mailwell Label). Clare Chapman, a true professional who grew and developed into an A-player, added to and helped shape many of these ideas.

These ideas played out on a larger plane with the opportunity for me to head HR at ADT Security Services, Inc., reporting to a true leader. Applying these ideas, I believe, played a key role in the dramatic turnaround of ADT Security Services, under the leadership of Steve Ruzika. Having the opportunity to work on a day-to-day basis with Ray Gross and Paul Lucking made a difference. The outstanding senior HR team we assembled at ADT included Mike Esposito, Jacquie Marshall, Jay Kirksey, Hal Johnson, and Stacey Childress. They were all strong and talented A-players who implemented this process (and others), with everyone playing key roles in the success of ADT. We all found out clearly that it is more fun (and profitable) to work with A-players.

Some colleagues in executive search have always been supportive of my efforts and have acted as excellent sounding boards. For me, I have truly valued their perspective and willingness to test ideas and supply feedback. Ernest Taylor and Joe Haberman of A.T. Kearney, Tom Zay of Zay-IIC Partners, Dick Slayton of Slayton International, and Terry Gallagher of Battalgia-Winston are all individuals who are stocking organizations with A-players . . . they are asked to make a difference and do so.

Introduction

Assessing the Personal Change Capacity of Your People

Change happens one person at a time. This doesn't mean you must identify the change capacity of thousands of employees one person at a time. It means that you must assess the capacity of the key people you're considering for pivotal positions in a change strategy. At its core, this process revolves around the following premise:

> Before change can happen, you need to assess your key people early on, and do so quickly, accurately, and with an eye toward new and emerging organizational requirements.

As simple as this sounds, it's rarely done. People make all sorts of false assumptions about an individual's readiness for change, ability to lead it, and capacity for performing within a changed system. In the rush to change, managers and human resources (HR) departments fail to assess whether people are really capable of carrying out new strategies or working in new ways. As a result, they don't make the right decisions about whom to develop, whom to transfer, whom to bring in from the outside, and whom to let go.

The process presented will help you make fast, accurate assessments of every key individual and ultimately make the right development decisions for the business. You'll gain a way to create a quantifiable display of your key people's change-related strengths and weaknesses that will greatly facilitate any change you need to make, whether it's transforming the entire business or revamping your small piece of it. You'll be able to make change-effective decisions from what you learn, both for your key people and for groups ranging from teams to entire organizations. As you'll discover, this is an especially useful tool not only for managers but for HR professionals who are often presented with seemingly impossible assignments related to change mandates. From attempting to identify individuals who will perform well in changing environments to developing change agents at higher levels, HR is presented with tough tasks that this process can facilitate.

The Neglected Square

To understand the importance of individual assessment, let's look at change from the vantage point of the change matrix shown in Figure I-1, which is a graphic representation of the four requisite activities involved in this process.

Figure I-1. Change Matrix

	Assessment	Development
Individual		
Organization		

As people plan and implement change programs, they tend to focus their efforts on the bottom two organizational squares. This is to be expected; change isn't going to be effective if the organization doesn't create and communicate a sound strategy or fails to implement a plan to deal with a flawed strategy. Though the individual development square receives some attention, it is usually in the form of cookie-cutter development programs that often bear little relationship to the change needs of an individual. And that's because the individual assessment square is either ignored or false assumptions are made. Individual assessment rarely is approached in a systematic manner, and it usually is the last and least important item on the change-management agenda. Instead, management makes broad, sweeping statements such as "Our people are . . ." or "Our managers are . . . ," assuming that change takes place in homogeneous groups.

What I'm suggesting is that individual assessment should be the first and most important item. This isn't to say that other factors aren't important. Issues such as strategy, alignment, financing, and technology all can play significant roles in a change effort.[1] Obviously, you're not going to change from a low-tech to a high-tech company unless you make an investment in new technology.

But all change roads lead back to people. You are not going to make an effective transition from a low-tech to a high-tech company unless the key people involved in the project embrace the new processes, as well as have the skills to capitalize on them and the leadership ability to motivate others to use the new equipment to the best of their abilities. No matter how process-oriented a change might be, people always have to implement it. The slogan from the old Fram oil filter commercial—"Pay me now or pay me later"—is applicable. If you don't assess people's change capacity up front, you'll have to do it later at a much greater cost.

This philosophy unfolds in three areas of implementation that will correspond to the three parts of this book:

1. *The Assessment Process* (Chapters 1 to 6). Six distinct steps will be described, each of which is designed to reveal

not only the personal change capacity of key individuals but the implications of that assessment for group or organizational change.

   2. *Creating a Development and Coaching Plan* (Chapters 7 to 10). The focus will be on helping you apply the vital information gleaned from individual assessments to make decisions about the roles people should play in implementing change. These chapters also will show you how to use development tools to increase personal change capacity so your employees can fulfill these roles effectively.

   3. *Organizational Readiness, Individual Action* (Chapters 11 and 12). Once you've created individual development plans to facilitate change-readiness, you need to look at the organizational issues that will affect those plans. These issues include strategy, people, processes, and implementation. Given this organizational assessment, you need to figure out what you can do to improve the organization's ability to increase change capacity (or what you can do within your area of responsibility).

   The relative lack of space devoted to organizational assessment and development is not meant to denigrate these essential tasks. Much has been written about organizational change-management strategy, and there is no need to cover the same ground.[2] Because there is so little awareness of and knowledge about individual change capacity assessment and development, we need to focus on these neglected topics. The organizational issues will be addressed in light of individual change capacity needs.

   I also want to emphasize that the path to organizational change is through individual change. The point of this process is not just to help a few, selected people become change leaders. As you'll see in the ensuing chapters, the impact of this process is cumulative. The goal, ultimately, is to create a critical mass of people who embrace and push change. By creating this critical mass, you greatly increase organizational change capacity.

   With this process structure in mind, let's begin with an

overview of the six steps that will guide your individual assessment efforts.

From Personal to Group Change Capacity

The goal of individual assessment is not to create a detailed, change-focused psychological profile. Not only would this profile be time-consuming to produce, but it would be filled with extraneous information. Even the most assiduous human resources (HR) leader doesn't need to know that someone's fear of change is rooted in his family's constant relocation when he was a small child. Instead, the goal of this first part of the process is to take a snapshot of an individual's change capacity and move to a group portrait. Put another way, the objective is to establish an aggregate change capacity. To make change happen in a work group, department, or organization, you need the sum total of all your personal change capacity assessments. In this way, you obtain crucial information about whether a given group possesses the capacity to lead and support a given change or will they fall short.

When you've completed the individual assessment process, you'll know how your group breaks out into A-, B-, C-, or D-players and how to interpret the mix of letter players. If you are an executive charged with changing your organization, you'll be able to assemble crucial data about the weak links, pivotal positions, towering strengths, and other factors that influence personal change capacity. When you've completed your individual assessment, you'll be able to create a development and coaching plan with confidence and knowledge, helping key players in ways that will let them contribute their best efforts to a change strategy.

I should also note that this process is fast. Certainly the speed at which you assess people depends on the number of people you're assessing; it obviously takes longer to assess all the key players in a Fortune 100 corporation than it does the pivotal people in the manufacturing division of a small company. Still, personal change capacity assessments for people in a midsize company can be done in a matter of weeks. This process is designed to help you get quick reads of people without in-depth interviewing and research. If you are like most managers or HR specialists, you're facing changes that are moving toward you quickly, and you don't have much time to get people ready.

Therefore, let's not waste any more time and start examining the six steps of the individual assessment phase of the process:

1. Evaluating five factors
2. Spotlighting two key measures—change response and versatility ratings
3. Creating profiles
4. Identifying group change capacity
5. Analyzing weak links
6. Drawing the roadmap

Figure I-2 will help you see how these steps flow together and the chapters in which they will be discussed at length.

Step 1: Evaluating Five Factors

Individual assessment begins by assembling a team of people you believe are best qualified to evaluate a given group. This assessment can be initiated as part of an HR effort, or it can be done independently by a manager concerned about his group's change capacity. In either case, the process generally is more effective with a few people on the assessment team, and a mix of managerial and HR assessors can often be useful. This is especially true if you have a significant number of key people—twenty or thirty—whom you need to evaluate. Even if you are only concerned with a few individuals, however, it's worthwhile to bring in at least two knowledgeable people who can provide you with an objective assessment.

Objectivity is crucial. If you are the only person evaluating an individual, it's likely your perspective will be biased, consciously or not. You are slaves to your experiences with this individual, experiences that are necessarily limited. In addition, if this person is a direct report, you've probably worked

Figure I-2. Overall Assessment Process

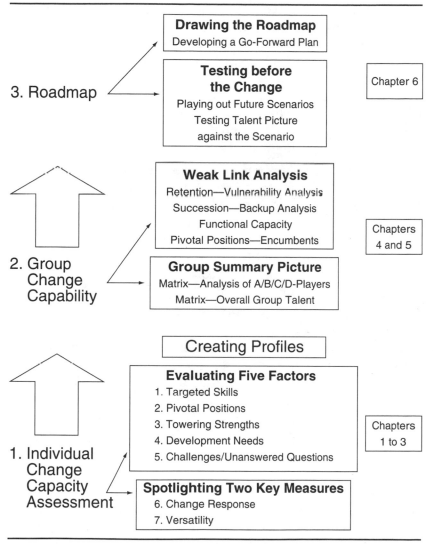

so closely together that it is difficult to gain the perspective necessary for objective evaluation. A mixed team of HR specialists and managers can challenge opinions with one another, debating and discussing an individual in order to arrive at a consensus; their combined knowledge of this person also is a significant advantage.

Once you've brought your team together, you need to discuss key people relative to five factors. The first two factors—targeted skills and pivotal positions—are external to the individual, requiring an assessment of the skills and positions your group (or the organization) deems critical. Three other factors—towering strengths, development needs, and challenges/unanswered questions—are internal and focused on an individual's personal qualities and issues. Let's briefly summarize what each of these five factors entails:

▲ *Targeted skills.* These are the skills that will be absolutely essential for a change strategy to be implemented effectively. What type of expertise will help your group execute its part of the strategy? From an HR perspective, what skills will be highly valued by the organization as it changes? Managers sometimes fail to project the new skills that their people will need to possess and are caught short when the time comes for them to execute their part of the strategy.

▲ *Pivotal positions.* Certain positions matter more than others from a change perspective. It may be that the position of plant manager is absolutely crucial for one change strategy while the HR director is pivotal for another. It is important to know what these pivotal positions are in advance because the individuals currently occupying these positions must possess strong personal change capacities. If not, you may have to find someone else for the job.

▲ *Towering strengths.* Given the targeted skills, do your people's towering strengths match up? This match is not as easy to assess as it might appear. For one thing, there is often a debate about what constitutes a towering strength. Sometimes team members confuse a run-of-the-mill strength with a towering one. For another, the match between targeted skill and towering strength may not be exact. For instance, the skill required might be marketing expertise while the towering strength is advertising savvy. Determining whether the match suffices for a group's change goals is an important task.

▲ *Development needs.* Sometimes it's obvious exactly what someone needs to learn or do in order to help a change effort. In these instances, it is important to note this need from the beginning of the process so that it can be addressed later. Other times, however, the team should explore this issue and determine if a development need is related to a planned change strategy. It may be a need that won't affect how an individual responds to change and thus doesn't need to be addressed. While development will be addressed in much greater detail in the second part of this process (Part Two: Creating a Development and Coaching Plan), the information that will inform development decisions is conducted in this first phase. HR professionals often are valuable contributors in this regard, since they are skilled at creating and implementing developmental programs; they often appreciate the importance of assessing development needs from a change capacity standpoint.

▲ *Challenges/unanswered questions.*[3] Many managers downplay these questions or challenges, figuring they'll resolve themselves on their own. They include personal developmental issues (Can John become more strategic in his thinking?) and key business issues (Can Mary grow the eastern region?). They might also involve questions about whether someone is going to remain with the organization for more than a year or whether another person can get over a personal problem and refocus his energy on work. If you are counting on someone to carry a major load during a change initiative, however, you can't ignore these questions and challenges. They need to be raised during the assessment process and addressed before someone is entrusted with a major role.

Step 2: Spotlighting Two Key Measures—Change Response and Versatility Ratings

Change response and versatility have the greatest impact on someone's change capacity. In one sense, the five factors provide you with insight about the issues that might affect someone's response to change and that person's value to your specific change effort. However, these two key measures identify someone's intrinsic ability (or inability) to deal with change:

▲ *Change response.*[4] Change response is the measure of an individual's past willingness and ability to learn from experiences and subsequently modify his behavior based on lessons learned. People who are highly willing and able to learn from experience respond positively to change; they quickly pick up on the new requirements in a changing workplace and embrace projects that call for them to work and lead in different ways.

▲ *Versatility.* Versatility, on the other hand, is future-focused. It is a speculative measure of an individual's ability to play an expanded role as her group or company evolves. As the word implies, *versatility* is about being able to adapt and take on different roles as change dictates. Unlike change response, the focus of the versatility rating is on making an educated guess about how someone might behave in a changing environment. How might Sue respond if we gave her a larger role as we shift to a team-based culture? How might George react if we gave him additional responsibilities during the transition period after the merger?

After you assess people relative to change response and versatility and filter in the five factors, you are able to view them in a new context. In the past, you may have conducted performance reviews or directly observed them in action, but you never evaluated them specifically in regard to change. Or you may have had a sense of how individuals responded to change but lacked a systematic way of translating this sense into usable data. If you are an HR professional, you've probably been frustrated with the instruments your organization uses to recruit and select change agents, recognizing that these instruments weren't designed for this purpose. This personal change capacity assessment provides you with very usable and tangible information, as the next step demonstrates.

Step 3: Creating Profiles

Profiles are a technique for organizing and analyzing the information you've collected. Profile forms enable you to enter information in ways that give you a clear picture of someone's personal change capacity. More important, they serve as a catalyst to fill in blanks you might have missed during your team meeting and to reassess conclusions that might not be accurate. For instance, you may find that someone with a high change-response rating has only a moderate versatility rating. During the initial assessment process, you may not have thought much of this incongruity, but now you might question why someone who responded so well to change in the past isn't likely to be particularly flexible in the future. You may determine that your versatility doubts relate to an unanswered question about the individual. This profile, therefore, lets you compare and contrast the five factors and two measures. The relationship between the factors may provide you with insights about an individual's change capacity.

While there are many possible profiles, six basic types predominate, ranging from someone who has strong change-response/versatility scores to a person with low change-response/versatility. These six types are discussed in Chapter 3. It's useful to start thinking of people in terms of these profile types; they give you a sense of where someone is located on the personal change capacity continuum. I've found that these profiles are especially useful for HR purposes, providing a catalogue of "snapshots" that can be pulled together and accessed quickly whenever someone requests change capacity information about a given individual.

Step 4: Identifying Group Change Capacity

With your profiles completed, you can now start looking at them as a group rather than in isolation. When plotted on a matrix, you clearly see your human assets (and liabilities) when it comes to change. You can determine if you are loaded with people who are highly versatile and respond well to change or if you're bottom-heavy with low change responders and inflexible individuals. While it is still too early in the process to determine exactly what you should do regarding individual development, you can obtain a good first impression of your group's readiness for change. By identifying your group change capacity, you can glimpse if you are going to have to go outside for talent, do more intensive development internally, or move people around (so that people with a high change capacity occupy pivotal positions).

This step is done to determine whether your people are A-, B-, C-, or D-players. With that written, a few words of warning are in order. At work as in school, grades are an oversimplification of an individual's achievement and potential for achievement, albeit a necessary assessment tool. Letter grades are best used in this step to assess the overall change capacity of your group rather than categorically rate an individual; you want to figure out the sum total of A-players you have versus D-players, for instance. Later on, you'll refine individual letter ratings based on additional information, so you need to take these initial letter grades with a grain of salt. For now, they serve as a catalyst for discussion of group capacity issues, including:

▲ Do you have the cumulative talent to accomplish your change goal?
▲ What are the best roles for each individual in a changing environment, given the change-based strengths and weaknesses of the group?
▲ What are the needs of specific individuals (e.g., coaching, rotation through different jobs) that will ensure they make a contribution to the changing group?
▲ Which people shouldn't be part of the group?

Step 5: Analyzing Weak Links

You now have turned the individual change capacity assessments into something that's relevant to your particular group's needs. But before you start making development decisions, you need to look at the change capacity of your people in a broader context. Weak links may exist at the periphery of your knowledge. As much as you may think you know about the individuals who work under your direction, there's a limit to your knowledge, especially if you are responsible for many individuals. Vulnerabilities lurk in the corners of what you don't know, and these weak links can affect your decisions about who should lead change and who needs to be developed. HR professionals often have the objectivity and training needed to spot these weak links, but they are sometimes frozen out of the assessment process, resulting in flawed assessments.

For instance, one organization was convinced that it was well-prepared to revamp its entire software system because the head of information technology (IT), Steven, was brilliant technologically and also a superb communicator and leader. Though he wasn't assessed using the personal change capacity tools described, he was certainly an A-player with strong change-response and versatility ratings. As the company began installing the new software, communicating its benefits, teaching everyone to use it, and ironing out the bugs, the entire process suddenly came to a standstill. Millions of dollars were lost, morale plummeted, and it took a full year before things were running smoothly again.

What happened? Steven left the company, and it discovered that Steven's backups were woefully unprepared to take over his role in this changing environment.

This was the weak link, the flaw that threw the organization's change process off the track. Most large groups in companies have at least one weak link (and oftentimes more), and it behooves your team to identify what that weak link is and, in the following roadmap step, take action to shore it up.

Weak links that can undermine your personal change capacity assessments include:

Functional capacity. Many change efforts require that certain functions be stronger than others. For example, let's say your change goal is a complete overhaul of back-office operations designed to take two or three years. A strong financial or IT function is crucial to implement the change project.

To test whether this might be a weak link, you must determine if you have sufficient depth in areas crucial to your change effort, or if you have enough people with towering strengths in these areas to ensure that the change program is planned and implemented smoothly and efficiently.

Pivotal position capacity. The focus is on the gap between what's needed for pivotal change positions and the capabilities of the incumbents who currently occupy these positions. If sales managers are crucial for a planned strategy and only one out of ten people occupying those positions ranks high in versatility and change response, then there's a potentially fatal lack of depth at these positions.

Backup successors. It's naive to believe that everyone is going to make it through change "alive," especially if you are in charge of a large group of people. Some key players will either drop out (choosing to take another job or retire) or find that they're not up to the task at hand (in which case they may be fired or transferred to another position). Backups for pivotal positions are essential, and you need to look at whether the backups have the personal change capacity necessary to step in and assume key roles.

In companies that I've been involved with, the typical backup ratio is as follows:

20 percent	Solid fit with the company's change needs
50 percent	Misfits (i.e., refers to people who are not ready to take on a role today, though they may be in the future with the right training and coaching; it may also be that they are ready to move, but are being blocked by someone who refuses to move on or out)
30 percent	Just do not fit

If your team finds itself faced with these common percentages, then alarm bells should ring. If you move forward with your change plans without acquiring additional bench strength, you are placing a lot of the burden for change on relatively few capable shoulders.

Talent vulnerability. You may have loads of people with the right personal change capacity for your strategy, but a red flag should wave if you are vulnerable to losing them. You need to assess how your A-players feel about the company (i.e., are they loyal or ambivalent?) and how marketable they are. For instance, they may have high change capacity but no interest in using it to its fullest, or if they are highly marketable, they may leave before they have a chance to use it. If you are vulnerable, you need to create a plan to "re-recruit" your people as well as to increase their compensation (and tie it to achieving change-based goals).

Step 6: Drawing the Roadmap

Once you have your group change capacity in place and are aware of your weak links, the next step is to discuss what actions to take in light of what you've learned.[5] In essence, your team needs to ask this question: "Given the implications of the change capacity of people in our group and the related weaknesses, what should we do to move in the direction of effective change?"

This final step in the individual assessment phase is designed as a transition to individual development. Although you're not going to be detailing specific development plans for individuals just yet, you are going to map out feasible directions for your key people that will influence your development plans. What you essentially want to do is determine how and if each person assessed can best contribute to your change strategy, and you can do this by looking at two areas:

1. *Future scenarios.* Where is the organization heading? What does your division, team, or group need to do to get there? In light of the information gleaned from your human asset inventory, what should you do to achieve your group's change goals? These and other questions need to be answered so that you don't just sit on the valuable information you've unearthed. A plan needs to be developed not only to achieve

your change goal, but to move you through the three other quadrants of the change matrix (Figure I-1).

2. *Individual staffing actions.* Based on a discussion of future scenarios, you need to decide what to do with your people. Some of them may be ready now to step in and lead your change effort. Others might be ready soon, given the right development. Still others may only be capable of carrying out their technical responsibilities and are incapable of furthering a change project—you need to make sure they aren't responsible for a major piece of the puzzle. Still others pose a threat to what you're trying to accomplish and must be transferred or let go. Specifically, you need to decide who will:

▲ Play a significant or larger role
▲ Stay in place and make a solid contribution
▲ Require coaching and other training so they "get on the program," as companies such as General Electric, Baxter, ADT, and NationsBank put it
▲ Have to be moved out of your group or the organization

An Amazingly Simple, Fast Process

On paper, this process appears more time-consuming than it actually is. Although the first phase has six steps, they can be taken quickly, sometimes in a matter of days (depending on how many people are being assessed). Assessing the personal change capacity of people is a highly intuitive, commonsense activity. With a bit of discussion, you and your team will reach consensus about who has had problems responding to change in the past and who has responded well. You'll discover that it is relatively easy to project who will eagerly and expertly assume new roles and responsibilities in the future and who will lack this versatility. The key is to have a *process* to discuss people. The content is there, the process in most organizations is missing. This approach solves the problem.

You'll find this assessment to be fast and easy because it uses a systematic process that guides your discussion and analysis. Too often, people are trying to assess an individual's readiness for change without a systematic process; consequently, managers and HR people become confused about what to do with their opinions and conclusions. The following chapters offer many reference points to help you keep your bearings. You'll also receive tips and techniques to help you get past the places where managers sometimes become stuck in their assessments.

Given all this, let's look at how to assess personal change capacity beginning with step 1, evaluating five factors.

Part One
The Assessment Process

1

Evaluating Five Factors

Assessing personal change capacity begins with an examination of five change-related factors, and it's an examination you need to get right to keep the rest of the process on track. It is all too easy to make false assumptions about individuals as well as to leave questions about them unanswered, thereby tainting the process. As a result, you'll incorrectly evaluate people crucial to your change effort. These evaluations may not be wildly inaccurate, but they may be faulty enough to sabotage a given strategy. For instance, you'll assume that someone has a towering strength crucial for your change strategy, but in reality it's only a fair-to-middling skill. Or you'll overlook the fact that an individual needs to work on a particular weakness or develop in a certain way before she's capable of assuming a pivotal change position.

Before analyzing the five considerations that will help you avoid these mistakes, let's briefly look at the evaluation team you need to put together to conduct this analysis.

Assembling an Evaluation Team

The team you put together will reflect your position within the organization and the piece of the change strategy you are charged with implementing. If you are a human resources (HR) person, you may have been charged with organizing and facilitating a special-purpose team; you've been asked to help assess people in a particular division or form a team that will assess people for specific change leadership positions. On the other hand, if you're a CEO attempting to transform an organization, the composition of your team will be different. Likewise, if you are a first-level manager or manager of managers with the objective of implementing some piece of a larger change program, your team will be different from both the HR professional's or the CEO's. The first-level manager's team may be able to evaluate its ten key people very quickly, whereas the CEO-catalyzed team may have hundreds of people to assess over a longer time frame.

Despite these differences, all evaluation teams are chosen in basically the same way. Prospective team members should meet the following criteria:

▲ *They must know the individuals in question.* For instance, your direct reports would be on a team that would evaluate their direct reports. Some familiarity with an individual's work performance is useful (though it's often a good idea to have a team member who doesn't work directly with the assessed individuals, such as an HR professional, providing a perspective that isn't biased by the politics and pressures of daily interactions).

▲ *They should have a vested interest in the change strategy's success.* This means that they'll take the assessment process seriously and recognize what your group needs to do to make change happen.

▲ *They should be individuals without an axe to grind.* You need people you can trust to be honest and objective, rather than those who are likely to play politics or favorites.

Pick your team members carefully because personal change capacity assessment is a delicate process. If a team member lacks necessary knowledge or is biased in some way, it will throw the assessment off. Inadvertently or maliciously, one team member can overestimate or underestimate someone's change capacity and taint the overall assessment. Therefore, don't be afraid to remove people from the team if you suspect they are hurting the process. Watch for patterns: Do your team members always talk positively about the direct reports they socialize with? Do they downgrade individuals who are aggressive and on the fast track? Do they consistently demonstrate an ignorance of people's behaviors and attitudes? Are they always negative in their assessments? These patterns suggest that a team member is not conducting an assessment properly.

The number of people you choose for the team will vary depending on the number of people you're assessing. Although there's no hard-and-fast rule about how many people constitute a good evaluation team, you want at least two people if you are assessing a small number of individuals and at least four or five team members if it is a large group.

As you convene your team, you need to make two things clear:

1. *Your assessment of an individual should not be biased for or against based on age, title, organizational level, area of expertise, tenure, or any other factor.* Certain prejudices and assumptions are common. For instance, older people are more resistant to change, or people at the top of the organization are very versatile. In fact, many young people are tremendously resistant to change and many top executives rigidly reject new and expanded assignments.

2. *Don't rely on traditional performance and promotability measures to predict personal change capacity.* Overreliance on performance ratings and promotability data is common, especially when it comes to choosing change leaders. In reality, people may have strong skills in a given area and exceed performance objectives but have great difficulty adapting to a new system or taking on unfamiliar responsibilities. Similarly, just because someone is ready to be promoted doesn't mean he's ready to handle the expanded role of a pivotal change position. In addition, change is future-oriented whereas performance ratings are present-oriented (i.e., these are the skills Mary performs well now). Performance ratings do not provide any indication of how well someone will master new skills or perform in a different environment. Finally,

organizations routinely overrate their people, as many in the
HR department are aware. At Quaker Oats, 88 percent of the
employees were rated at "above average," and I've found similarly high figures at other organizations. So even if performance ratings equaled personal change capacity, it would not
be a valid measure.

For these reasons, I discourage bringing performance appraisals into change capacity assessment sessions. I would
much rather solicit the opinions of team members and arrive
at a consensus than be restricted by the biases of performance
appraisals. In fact, these performance instruments can actually
deflect the discussion away from change capacity and focus
attention on secondary issues such as skill sets, selection, and
compensation.

This doesn't mean that past performance is irrelevant to
personal change capacity assessments. People who have demonstrated superior performance may be the type of individuals
who will excel at any task, whether or not it's change-related.
Past performance is also a valuable factor in determining an
individual's towering strength; it may indicate that Steve is an
information technology (IT) expert or that Linda has top-level
communication skills. While this is valuable information,
teams shouldn't overvalue it. Performance ratings can be de-
ceptive when it comes to personal change capacity.

The factors that you and your team will evaluate are as
follows:

1. Targeted skills
2. Pivotal positions
3. Towering strengths
4. Development needs
5. Challenges/unanswered questions

Let me offer you two final pieces of advice to help your
team assess these factors quickly and accurately:

1. *Discussion rather than formal presentations will facilitate your team's progress.* One of the biggest mistakes evalua-

tion teams make is thinking that they need to prepare exhaustive psychological studies on each person, and that they must offer lectures on the strengths or deficiencies of a particular individual. Not only do these long-winded speeches and accompanying written materials bog down discussion, but they require a lot of time.

2. *Personal change capacity is entirely different from psychological change capacity.* The process I'm describing works precisely because it cuts through all the side issues and mountains of psychological testing and gets to the heart of the matter fast. I've seen groups debate for days or even weeks on an individual's capacity to lead or manage change (and still get it wrong in the end). As you'll learn, if you take a clear snapshot of the traits described here, you can determine change capacity with great speed.

Let's begin with the first two factors on our list—targeted skills and pivotal positions—since they are external to the individual and therefore you need to examine these factors in advance of your initial team meeting.

Targeted Skills

Before your team meets, you need to schedule a session with your boss or someone in senior management who can help you define the key skills and pivotal positions that will be crucial in the future. If you are an HR team member, then you may already be privy to this information. If you don't possess this information, talk with the right individual (or get input from two or three others) so that you have a sense of what competencies are going to drive the change (or changes) that the organization is going to undergo and what positions will be absolutely essential to make these changes work. With this knowledge, you can tailor your personal change analysis to fit the needs of your evolving environment. You'll be immediately aware that Joe is ill-suited or well-suited for a key change position because of the skills he lacks or possesses.

The following questions will help you create a list of two or three skills clusters:

1. *Who is the organization's best performer/leader of change?* The idea is to identify the prototype, the person who currently possesses the skills that will be critical to the company as it changes. Grounding the skills in reality rather than in an ideal composite is a good way to start out. When you ask a senior manager a question about skills, she'll find it easier to answer if she can point to a person who embodies these skills rather than having to come up with a list from scratch. HR often does surveys or collects information related to this issue and may be in a good position to answer this question.

2. *What is this person doing that other people are not?* This question is a good test of why someone's particular skills are important to achieve change goals. What are the specific competencies that this individual possesses that allow him to lead, achieve, and innovate in ways that others cannot?

3. *If we could choose the skills that would make a positive difference for our change effort in the future, what would they be?* After anchoring a skills list in reality, it is fine to engage in some blue-sky thinking. What would an ideal list of change skills look like? If the ideal list differs from the real skills list you've created, are the ideal skills reasonable for us to ask someone to possess or develop, especially within a limited time frame?

Based on these three questions and relatively brief discussions with a senior executive, make a targeted list of skills. It is fine to discuss this list with your team, but don't overthink it or try for 100 percent precision. All you need is a sense of what skills will prove valuable for your company's change goals.

Traps to Avoid

In compiling this list, watch out for the following traps:

▲ *Dwelling on past rather than future skills.* What helped the company become successful might not be the same skills required to achieve success in the future. Don't compile a list that only reflects past skills; ask senior people to factor in five-year plans and more immediate strategies to create the targeted skills.

▲ *Focusing primarily on technical skills.* Although technical skills certainly are important, they should not comprise more than 30 percent of your list. In most change efforts, leadership skills involving people, strategy, and tactics deserve greater emphasis. It's especially easy, however, to fall into this trap when a change goal is focused on one particular area—becoming more sales driven, for example, or improving technologically—then everyone becomes obsessed with sales and technology skills.

▲ *Creating too many targeted skills.* When you've compiled a list of twenty or thirty skills, it becomes cumbersome to work with. As you are evaluating the personal change capacity of your people, you may begin struggling to keep track of all the skills; you'll also get confused about which ones should be prioritized. At Federal Express, CEO Fred Smith created the mantra of "people, service, and profitability," which served as a basis for the skills that employees needed to possess or develop. A simple framework for the skills you require—perhaps two or three umbrella terms that describe the skills—will make your team's job that much easier.

▲ *Turning a simple task into a complex procedure.* I've seen managers get carried away with creating lists of competencies or HR people who rely on some intricate formula for arriving at competency clusters. They've commissioned lengthy studies, hired consulting firms, and spent many dollars and hours on identifying every possible skill that will be of use to support, catalyze, and lead change. You shouldn't make the process complex or time-consuming. Good input from a senior-level person and a brief discussion among team members should suffice. You may miss a skill or two, but as long as you establish a good general framework, it will be effective.

Pivotal Positions

Identifying pivotal positions is also an important premeeting task, though it is not one you need to spend much time on in the beginning. Later, toward the middle of this individual assessment process, you'll need to become more specific about your pivotal positions (Chapter 3 will provide tips and techniques for creating profiles). At this point, however, you simply want to start considering what positions can make or break your piece of the change effort. Once you know the personal change capacity of the people you are assessing, you have a tremendous opportunity to place A-players in these pivotal positions (you also have the chance to make sure C- and D-players aren't in these positions).

The biggest problem with identifying pivotal positions is as follows:

> Everyone on your team will insist that just about every position is pivotal.

This is human nature, or it's the nature of managers who may honestly believe that they can't implement any change without tremendous contributions from each and every one of their people. If you are an HR professional, you probably are better able to differentiate pivotal from nonpivotal positions because you don't have the same direct involvement as other managers. If you are not in HR, you may need help from senior management so you can accurately designate pivotal positions. Ask your boss or the HR member of your team about the positions that will become increasingly important as a new strategy is implemented. It may be that a position that was essential but not critical for many years suddenly becomes pivotal because of a specific change strategy.

For instance, when Federal Express was a start-up company, frontline people such as customer service agents and couriers were absolutely, positively critical to the company's success in making its new approach to overnight delivery work. Later on, the pivotal positions shifted to IT managers as the company changed the way it serviced an expanded distribution system.

Towering Strengths

Your team should begin by identifying the one, two, or three towering strengths possessed by the person under discussion.[1] Right from the start, make it clear to the group that any more than three towering strengths are too many—few people possess more than three such strengths, and usually any number beyond this amount reflects things people are competent at rather than tremendously skilled at.

As the term implies, a *towering strength* conveys true expertise. In your discussion, don't confuse towering strengths with either middle-of-the-road competencies or personality traits. In meetings, I've heard people talk about John's "likability" or Mary's "intelligence." What you are looking for are highly prized skills, often ones that are uniquely John's or Mary's. For instance, a towering strength might be an ability to craft a vision and communicate it in a motivating way; another strength might be an uncanny knack for coming up with the right innovative idea at the right time; still another might be brilliance at organizing teams and getting them to work together synergistically. Don't feel constrained by the standard list of skills and competencies; towering strengths come in all shapes and sizes.

Many times, it is relatively easy for a team to achieve consensus about a towering strength. It may take seconds for everyone to agree that Steven is a brilliant strategist. On the other hand, if you encounter disagreement, can't narrow the list down to under three strengths, or can't come up with any strengths at all, keep the following tips in mind:

▲ *Recognize that not everyone has a towering strength.* You can neither squeeze water from a stone nor a towering strength from a solid citizen. Organizations are filled with people who are competent at many things but spectacular at none of them. If this seems to be the case, don't waste time trying to invent a strength when it doesn't exist.

▲ *Remain specific and focused; you are probably off-track if you find yourself with five or ten towering strengths per person.* People tend to trade on reputations—"Everyone knows that Gary is terrific at working cross-functionally." When your team members make general statements such as this, ask for examples and time frames when these events took place. Some people may once have been great at some endeavor, but their skills have become rusty. When the discussion is concrete and time-sensitive, the number of towering strengths naturally reduces to a realistic number.

▲ *Be wary of "one of our best" statements.* This might be true, but it's the wrong measure of a towering strength. Your barometer should be external rather than internal. In other words, is it a towering strength when examined in a larger context? Is Sally really one of the best leaders around, or is she only average when compared with leaders in other organizations? Make sure "one of our best" is one of everyone's best. Play devil's advocate and question whether the team is over-rating someone because "he's the best we've got."

Once you've agreed upon an individual's towering strengths, note how they match up with the list of targeted skills you created before the meeting. You might want to place an asterisk next to matches between skills and strengths; this will alert you that this particular personal change capacity includes a towering strength that might be especially useful for a given change initiative.

Development Needs

It may be apparent to everyone on the team that the person under discussion needs to work on a particular skill, especially in light of the skills that will be required as the company transforms itself. Getting this need on the table is a significant element in the personal change capacity assessment process.

I've found that organizations that are just embarking on change programs (i.e., ones that maintained the status quo for years and years) often have no impetus to look at development in the broader sense of the term. Because the organization hasn't changed, job descriptions and skills needs have remained relatively constant. As a result, no one has pointed out to Joe or Mary that they are coming up short in some area that is beyond the requirements of their current jobs. In other organizations, there is simply a lack of candor: The boss isn't strong enough to point out a development need or the corporate culture eschews candor and constructive criticism in favor of politeness.

The key is to state whether someone has a development need, especially as it relates to the pivotal positions and targeted skills that have been determined to be crucial for change. An individual may have multiple development needs, and your team must prioritize them, focusing on the one or two that will have the most impact on the change strategy.

This development need might derail a few people who are under assessment.[2] Someone will simply come up short in a key area because he lacks the necessary talent or motivation, which will make it impossible for him to occupy a pivotal position in the change effort. Most needs, however, can be met with the right training (e.g., on-the-job or classroom). People often have average skills that they can improve upon through job rotations or development programs of some kind. Some individuals also are average in certain areas because they've lacked the opportunities to develop a particular skill (i.e., it wasn't needed in the past but it is now).

Perhaps the most important task at this point is to discuss whether a development need can be met within a reasonable time frame. Here is the make-or-break question:

> Can this person develop the skill required in time for it to be of use in making change happen?

A common mistake is to set up a development program for an individual that ultimately will be successful, but not in time to be of much use to the organization. By the time Joe has received the necessary training, worked with a coach, and developed a critical competency, it's too late—he isn't ready to contribute when his contribution is needed. If you are an HR person, you probably have a handle on the time it takes for someone to complete development in a given area. If you are with business management, rely on the expertise of the HR person on your team, or bring in someone from HR to help you make this assessment.

The other red flag to watch for is this:

> The development need requires someone to make a quantum leap in skill type.

In other words, an individual contributor needs to become a manager; a manager must become a manager of managers; a manager of managers must turn into a senior executive. If you foresee the development need for an individual, be forewarned that this need can't be met quickly or easily.

Challenges/Unanswered Questions

People have different challenges and questions that govern their behaviors that may ultimately impact how they lead change or react to it. The challenges are often related to someone's Achilles' heel—he is bafflingly inconsistent as a strategist, great on one project, awful on the next. As a result, this challenge trips this person up when change is involved. Similarly, a persistent, unanswered question about an individual may create problems. For instance, Sue may have a towering strength perfectly matched to a targeted skill, and she may be moved into a position pivotal to a change effort. The question that dogs Sue, however, is whether she's going to stay with the company; her towering strength makes her highly marketable. Just when the change program is unrolling, Sue leaves the company when she receives a great offer, and the change program stalls.

If your team can air these issues, it may be able to prevent disaster. During the team discussion, a question arises about

Sue's commitment to the company. The rumor is that she's a target of headhunters, and the team members agree that Sue needs to reaffirm her commitment to stay with the organization, at least during the next year or two, before they place her in a pivotal position.

Other times, however, this discussion about challenges and questions isn't done as much to head off disaster as to help people reach their maximum personal change capacity. Talking about the questions surrounding an individual provides valuable information that can be used to structure a development program geared to this individual's needs.

I've found that these discussions are productive when they revolve around "can" and "will" questions. The former is a skill question—"Can John master team building in time to help orchestrate the restructuring process?" The latter is a question of motivation—"Will Mary take on the responsibilities necessary to help her new group achieve its ambitious goals?"

Ask your team to formulate a number of can and will questions about an individual. The best way to start is to concentrate on one or more specific areas that are especially relevant to given individuals and the role they might play in a change program. The following are some sample questions from different areas:

People Issues

▲ Will Greg confront performance issues directly and push performance to a higher level when we roll out our new strategy?
▲ Can Barbara learn to negotiate and compromise with others—a skill she's going to need in spades after the merger—or will she always try to win at any cost?

Service Issues

▲ Can Bob continue to provide strong leadership when the situation becomes much more ambiguous?
▲ Will Russ shift from an operational/short-term mindset to a more strategic point of view?

▲ Can Denise refocus the unit on key customer retention objectives after the restructuring?

Profitability Issues

▲ Can Joan reestablish our customer base if we give her more opportunities to use her influence and implement her ideas?
▲ Can Susan take the start-up and quickly show that it is going to be profitable, even though she's been somewhat slow and methodical in the past (when speed wasn't a priority)?

One of the most common mistakes teams make when raising unanswered questions is to raise them from the perspective of the organization. For instance, Can the company take advantage of Bob's leadership ability in a more ambiguous environment? This is a good question, but it's tangential to the purpose. Right now your team is concerned with the personal change capacity of the individual. You want to discover whether Bob's ability to respond to change and take on roles of greater scope and scale is at all compromised by the problems he might have with ambiguity; you want to discover what development needs Bob has that can better help him deal with ambiguity and thus change.

Establishing a Change Capacity Framework

People don't experience change in a vacuum. Environment and job-related issues affect an individual's capacity to deal with and drive change. These five considerations covered in this chapter relate to key aspects of someone's experience and environment. If someone's towering strength (job-related) matches up perfectly with his group's or organization's targeted skill (environment), then you've acquired a significant piece of information about this person's ability to contribute to the changes you need to implement. Recognizing that someone who occupies a pivotal position (environment) has a development need (job-related) puts you one step ahead of the game; you won't rely on this person to lead change until the appropriate development work is done. Addressing unanswered questions (job-related) avoids unpleasant surprises.

Once you've put this framework in place, you are ready to evaluate people's responses to change in the past and how versatile they might be in taking on new roles and responsibilities in the future.

2

Spotlighting the Two Key Measures of Change Response and Versatility

One way of looking at personal change capacity is as a combination of extrinsic and intrinsic factors. Whereas Chapter 1 focused on the extrinsic qualities, this chapter examines the two qualities that determine an individual's inherent ability to handle change. Although extrinsic factors are important, change response and versatility are the heart and soul of change capacity.

To a certain extent, assessing change response and versatility flows from your managerial experience with an individual or the records at your disposal as part of your human resources (HR) function. HR people tend to rely on data previously accumulated from performance reviews and interviews, and they jump to conclusions about change response and versatility. Similarly, if you are a manager and you've worked closely with someone, you may be tempted to deliver an assessment quickly based on your observations. In fact, I've seen team members arrive at response and versatility ratings in a matter of seconds. Sally has worked for and with team members for years, and they remember that she had no problem handling a radically new manufacturing system in the past; their gut tells them that she's sufficiently flexible that she'll eagerly assume whatever new roles and responsibilities a changing environment calls for.

Their first reaction might be absolutely right, and Sally may deserve a high rating in both change response and versatility. The process presented here is designed to help teams test their initial assessments. Change response and versatility can be a little tricky, so a formal, systematic approach helps avoid wrong guesses and selective memories.

Evaluating People in a Nontraditional Way

Although some people may come up with instant change-response and versatility assessments, most team members find this type of assessment to be a foreign experience. That's because everyone is trained to rate direct reports in terms of pure performance issues and not based on change capacity. No one is taught to differentiate how someone performs a familiar task compared with one that is unfamiliar. No one is asked to rate how a direct report responds in a static environment instead of a volatile one. Even HR professionals, who have more experience than most managers in the science of performance evaluation, often find change response and versatility to be a bit confusing initially.

Before focusing on the specifics of change response and versatility, I'd like you to try the following exercise. It is designed to help you become more accustomed to evaluating people based on their change capacity.

1. Write down the names of five people you know well; they can be people you work with, friends, or family. Next to each name, note a specific instance in which they were asked to make a significant change in their personal or work life. Describe how they reacted to change. Did they embrace it with enthusiasm, accept it reluctantly, vacillate between acceptance and resistance, or fight it with all their might? Give each person a letter grade for his or her response, with A being the grade for the greatest acceptance of change and D being the least acceptance.

2. Now pretend that you know that each of these five people is going to be facing an even greater amount of change in the future. To handle that change effectively, they will have to take on new roles, shift directions in their life, or demonstrate greater responsibility. Again, this future change doesn't have to be work-related. It may be that they'll have to move and learn to live in a new environment or that they'll get married to someone who already has kids and they've never been a parent. Speculate about how flexible each of them might be in handling a new role. Give them a numerical score between 1 and 5, with 1 representing the greatest versatility.

3. Look at the two ratings—the letter grade and the numerical score—and decide the following: Whom would you want to lead a change program in which you had a vested interest? Whom would you want to provide support? Who do you think might be capable of contributing leadership or support with a certain amount of training and coaching? Who won't contribute much or anything, no matter what you do? Who is likely to sabotage change?

Admittedly, this exercise is more simplistic than the evaluation your team would conduct. Nonetheless, the fundamental concept in this exercise is the same as the one you'll use to assess your people. Crossing past response to change with future versatility yields great insight about someone's personal change capacity. Even this simple exercise reveals that A-1 rated individuals will probably be great change leaders and those rated D-5 will obstruct any change that comes their way.

Change Response Rating

If you wanted to, you could spend days talking about how a given individual responds to change. Psychological testing can provide you with all sorts of subtle insights, offering explanations about why people respond to change as they do. As a psychologist, I use testing and would be the last person to suggest that it lacks merit. But psychological testing can be a slow, cumbersome process; it reveals more about the person than about the person's change capacity. If you delve too deeply into what makes a person tick, you become enmeshed in feelings about change and their origins and never get a good read on what actions a person takes in response to a changing environment. The goal is to get a quick read of an individual's personal change capacity, and the psychological subtleties aren't much help in that regard. You need to get a usable handle on how individuals have responded to change when confronted with it in the past. The following change response rating system will help you assign a rating quickly and accurately.

Active Responders

These individuals embrace change in an action-oriented, opportunistic way. Rather than playing it safe when faced with new and unfamiliar people, policies, and procedures, they are willing to think outside of the box. They also are highly receptive to other people's original thinking and are skilled at projecting how that thinking might play out in the real world. They bring a sense of urgency to the right issues; they don't become distracted by all the minor hassles associated with change or delay action because they're afraid to take risks. Instead, they move fast on major issues, heading straight for the difficult but key change challenges.

Identifying Trait of Active Responders

They are adept at and eager to learn from change-related experiences. This can mean that when they try to implement a change and their efforts fail, they don't expend their energy on covering their mistakes or finding someone or something to blame. Instead, they see the failure as an opportunity to gain knowledge and wisdom about change, and they subsequently articulate and use what they've learned.

Passive Responders

Though they respond positively to change, passive responders don't adjust personal, interpersonal, or managerial behaviors with the speed or enthusiasm of active responders. Sometimes they need direction to implement a change rather than leading the effort. These are not the people who will challenge the status quo. When push comes to shove—or when a change effort creates higher levels of stress and discomfort—they become malleable, doing what is politically expedient or safe rather than pushing through to the next level. They're good at adopting and adapting to change, and not so good at creating risk-taking ideas that accelerate change.

Identifying Trait of Passive Responders

They go with the flow, but they don't move people in new directions. Intellectually, they may realize that they have to make an unpopular decision or come up with a daring new idea to increase the odds of a change taking hold, but they're reluctant to translate their ideas into action. These people will support the change as long as it doesn't threaten them or demand that they demonstrate initiative.

Reactive Responders

These people manifest rigid, fixed patterns of behavior in the face of change. Although they can learn new ways of working, they're tough sells on new initiatives and drain their managers' energy as they try to convince them to buy into the new program. Here and there reactive responders might make some changes, but they certainly won't lead them or even show much initiative relative to whatever change is taking place. Typically, they change when forced to by dictum.

Identifying Trait of Reactive Responders

They are the ones who make management's collective hair turn white. They're frustrating to deal with because they often have the intelligence and skills necessary to contribute to a change program, but they choose not to use their capabilities unless they're browbeaten into it. When you find someone who in the past has had to be dragged kicking and screaming into using a new system or has made changes with agonizing slowness, reluctance, and complaints, you've found a reactive responder.

Blocked Responders

When it comes to change, these people demonstrate little liking for or willingness to accept anything new or different. When confronted with change, they often respond in one of two ways. Either they study problems into the ground and refuse to make decisions, or they make quick decisions to obliterate the ambiguity, conflict, and complexity that often accompany change. In either case, change causes them to act in unproductive and sometimes destructive ways. In some cases, blocked responders are habit-bound, perfectionistic, and overcontrolling: They react to change by holding tight to tradition and things they can control.

Identifying Trait of Blocked Responders

Probably the easiest way to spot blocked responders is to look for people who are unable to learn from their experiences. They seem to treat learning events as if they didn't happen. While the other three categories of people will take away something from an encounter with change, blocked responders literally block out the experience. You fully expect that they would have learned something from having gone through an upheaval at a former employer or having been part of a group that implemented a new policy or process. These people, however, exhibit the trait of obliviousness.

If you or people on your team have difficulty differentiating the four change-response categories, the following story will help:

> You've just hired Ann as a manager in your sales group, and you brief her on the volatile conditions in your industry. You explain that a number of new competitors from the Pacific Rim have entered the market and made strong in-

roads with their low-price strategy. To help combat these new competitors (as well as to deal with other changing market conditions), you ask her to study the situation and recommend a course of action quickly. Shortly thereafter, Ann comes up with a detailed strategy designed to combat low-price competitors as well as a comprehensive proposal to test-market this approach.

You're astonished not just with the speed, detail, and insights that Ann brought to the assignment, but with the fact that she came up with anything at all. You've asked others in your sales group to deal with this changing market, and so far, all you've received are rationalizations about how there's no way you can compete on price.

When Ann's concept is test-marketed, however, it isn't particularly effective. A number of customers continue to resist her quality-focused program. Even though you don't ask her to do it, Ann writes an analysis of why she believes the test failed and how it might be retested with a new structure in order to correct the flaws. Her belief is that the company's own salespeople weren't sufficiently motivated to sell the new quality concept to customers; they didn't understand the concept clearly and a training session that clearly communicates the rationale for the quality focus might do the trick. You accept Ann's idea, a retest takes place, and your company wins back a number of customers lost to foreign competitors.

Ann is an active responder not just because she came up with a successful new approach in a changing environment, but because she quickly learned from her experience and articulated a new strategy based on that learning.

Now let's say you take Ann's idea and talk

about it with Paul, another manager in your group. You ask Paul to help you analyze the results of Ann's test and come up with new ideas so that you can roll it out. After a month, Paul comes back with a brief report that endorses what Ann has done, explaining how it makes perfect sense to use her strategy as a model for a rollout. He suggests a few minor changes, but he fully endorses Ann's innovative concepts.

You think back about how Paul has responded to other challenges and changes in the past, and you conclude he usually responds this way. He's not afraid of change, and when he's called upon to do something in a different way he does so, adapting and adopting it a bit but basically embracing the strategy. Paul will do a solid job with the rollout, and you know you can count on his support and effort. On the other hand, he's not going to show a great deal of initiative or leadership—he'll just tweak the strategy a bit and push it forward at a measured pace.

As a solid citizen—someone who deals with change in a bland but dependable way—Paul is clearly a passive responder.

You know you need to talk to Russ, a sales manager for another region, about Ann's new approach, but you're not looking forward to it. Whenever you've suggested that Russ try something new or even think about something from a fresh perspective, he resists. This time is no different. He insists that his group tried something similar to what Ann did three years ago "and it didn't work." When you talk to Russ, his eyes glaze over and you can tell he's tuning out what you are trying to explain to him. Still, you ask him to give the concept a try. At your next meeting with Russ, however, it's clear that he's done nothing. This time he tells you that his group is already doing some of the things that Ann has tested, although you know this isn't the case. Again, you ask Russ to get to work on it. By the third meeting, you are no longer asking but telling. Only after you get in Russ's face and insist that he start implementing Ann's approach does he respond in the way that you need him to respond. He tells you that he didn't realize it was such an important issue, but now that he understands its importance he'll get right on it.

Russ is a reactive responder. He'll change only when push comes to shove.

Finally, you need to meet with Barbara, who has been with the company for twenty-three years and is firmly entrenched, delivering solid sales results year after year (though the results aren't quite as solid in recent years as they had been in the past). She is cynical about anything and everything, and Barbara's attitude has always been that "if I can survive quality circles and that CEO who was here less than a year, I can survive anything." Though Barbara listens politely when you talk to her about Ann's plan and doesn't overtly reject it, she also gives you a number of signals that she's not about to change her mode of operation. She gives you all sorts of excuses why she can't put the issue of Ann's test on her next staff meeting agenda and insists, "My plate is too full to even consider doing anything about it this year." Later, you hear that Barbara has been openly hostile when talking to her people about Ann's strategy, insisting that Ann doesn't know their customers and that "this too shall pass."

Barbara is a blocked responder. No matter how many times you meet with her and no matter how eloquent your arguments, she has no intention of changing any aspect of how she operates.

With this story, and keeping the earlier definitions in mind, your team can begin rating people. Sometimes this process is a snap; everyone immediately agrees that Barbara is a classic blocked responder. Other times, however, there's disagreement or lack of clarity on what constitutes an appropriate rating. Here are some of the more common situations you might encounter and what to do about them:

▲ *There's an inconsistent change response pattern.* It can be confusing when one member of the team talks about the great job John did implementing a policy change while someone else notes that John resisted a process change for months. To one person, John seems like an active responder while to another he seems to be a blocked responder. The truth is actually somewhere in between. To find this truth, the team needs to determine:

1. If someone generally responds positively to change except when the change represents a direct threat (to his position or power) or requires him to show initiative. If this is the case, he is probably a passive responder.
2. If someone responds positively to change only when pushed hard but otherwise resists it, she is probably a reactive responder.

▲ *Someone falls between the category cracks.* In other words, an individual is part active responder and part passive responder. In these instances, don't get hung up on this fact. These ratings aren't intended to be an exact science, and it won't taint your overall personal change capacity assessment if you are off by one category. If someone is on the cusp between categories, preface your designation with "high" or "low." If someone is squarely between active and passive, note that he's a low active responder or a high passive responder. As this process unfolds and you begin to make development decisions about what roles are appropriate for people, you can take this high or low qualifier into consideration. It may be that when you factor in other data—the versatility rating as well as the five factors from Chapter 1—you'll be in a better position to determine if someone belongs in the passive or active category.

▲ *The team believes an individual has great potential as a change leader but there's no evidence to back up this belief.* The mistake is to go with your wish rather than your experience. This happens when somebody is very likable, has come to the company highly recommended, or is simply someone who talks a good game when it comes to change. The change response rating, however, is rooted in observed behaviors and attitudes related to change. You need to rely on the combined observations of team members rather than their enthusiasm for a particular person.

Figure 2-1 provides a summary of each change response category.

Figure 2-1. Change Response

Today: How do we view this individual in terms of his or her response to change—what do we know of the person?

☐ **Active Responder:** Proactive; action-oriented; takes initiative; learns quickly when facing new, complex, or ambiguous situations

☐ **Passive Responder:** Not the first to grab the initiative, but can be counted on

☐ **Reactive Responder:** Only responds to dictates—a very tough sell, seen as resistant to change and rarely out in front of an issue

☐ **Blocked Responder:** Seen as habit bound, gives too many pat answers, definitely not a leader of change—blocks it more often than not

---

Versatility Rating

Whereas the change response rating is based on an individual's past reactions to specific situations, the versatility rating looks at future issues. Specifically, can the individual play a larger role in terms of scope and scale? Put another way: Will this person be sufficiently versatile to take on more and different responsibilities?

Scale and scope are the two measures you'll use to determine someone's versatility. Specifically:

▲ *Scale has to do with size.* For example, can Linda manage three regions in a changed system rather than just the one she's currently managing? As organizations restructure, merge, launch new processes, and the like, people are called upon to do more. Sometimes this involves a promotion; sometimes it's a function of an expanded role for the same or a similar position. While some people are sufficiently versatile that they can take on an expanded role with ease, others rigidly reject even a slight expansion of their duties.

▲ *Scope is a horizontal concept.* It entails a widening of responsibilities and the ability to handle new and varied assignments. In a changing system, people need to do different things. The manager who was responsible for sales now needs to become involved in marketing and customer service. The person who always worked alone now must work as part of a team. The domestic manager must learn to think globally. While some people may be highly versatile when it comes to scale, they may be inflexible when it comes to scope: They can do more, but they can't do new and different.

To help your team make an accurate assessment of an individual's versatility, here are some tips and techniques that will make your team's job easier.

Clearly Versatile Individuals

These people are eagerly awaiting the next challenge and are ready to assume a larger and broader role. In fact, if you don't feed these people a steady diet of new and different tasks, they'll leave and find an organization that will meet these needs.

To identify clearly versatile individuals, answer the following questions:

▲ When this person was given additional responsibilities in the past, did he grumble about the increased workload, accept it without grumbling openly but seemed to resent the added tasks, or assimilate the added responsibilities without missing a beat?

▲ When this person was given a new type of assignment or one that was deeper and broader in scope, did she get thrown for a loop and struggle with unfamiliar concepts, make a valiant effort to expand her role but seem uncomfortable with the new assignments, or seem almost chameleon-like in her ability to slip into and out of new and broader-based roles?

A good exercise for the team is to discuss possible new and broader roles that often accompany change and how an individual might handle them. For instance, talk about how someone might handle the situation if he were asked to:

▲ Manage twice the number of employees that he currently is responsible for
▲ Move from a functional to a cross-functional leadership position
▲ Change his management style (to become more open, more participatory, more team-oriented)
▲ Take on major new challenges such as becoming responsible for global markets or orchestrating a merger

In your discussion, you want to distinguish between those people whose versatility is such that they could immediately handle a position of greater scale and scope, and those who require a bit more seasoning before they could handle the position. Focus on whether someone has had a relatively narrow range of responsibilities and experiences up to this point. As versatile as some individuals in this group might seem, they probably need a broader range of experiences before they can take on a change leadership position. Next to each person's "clearly versatile" rating write an *R* for ready now and a *D* for development, in order to differentiate these two types.

Expandable/Versatile Individuals

People in this category are also quite versatile and will eventually be able to take on new, expanded roles in a changing company. The big question is when they'll be able to take on these roles. Some might be ready in less than a year whereas others might require more development over a longer period of time. You want to estimate if someone's development needs are moderate (M) or significant (S). While a certain amount of guesswork is involved, your team can determine how much work is necessary before someone is ready to take on a larger role by addressing the following questions:

- ▲ If you could add experience in any area for this person, where would it be?
- ▲ How might this lack of experience prevent this person from effective performance in a new and expanded role?
- ▲ How long does it typically take for someone to develop this experience?
- ▲ Is there a training program or other tool that might accelerate this process?

Don't underestimate the development needs and time frame of someone in this category. If you need someone to acquire difficult skills or let go of ingrained behaviors in order to take on new roles and responsibilities—and if you don't have an effective program in place to help her do so—then acknowledge that the development need is significant. Expandable/versatile individuals have great potential to contribute to a change effort, but don't mistake that potential for current reality. They're in this category because they don't yet have the capacity to handle the scope and scale of responsibilities that change will place upon them. They'll likely come up short if you give them too many new tasks or if you ask them to take on challenging and unfamiliar responsibilities.

When you are optimistic about an individual's potential for versatility but dubious about his ability to fulfill that potential in the near future, then that individual belongs in this category.

Irreplaceable Pro

This is often a highly talented individual who, from a technical skills standpoint, is crucial to whatever changes are planned. These pros are versatile within limits—usually the limits of their main skill sets.[1] While they might lack the versatility necessary to assume significantly different functions in the future, they should not be overlooked because their contributions will continue to be meaningful. That's why the team needs to make sure a development program is created that helps maintain this person's motivation and self-esteem and provides a growth path within a given technical area.

In most instances, irreplaceable pros are easy to identify; their reputations precede them. The key thing here is to determine if a technically superior person transcends her skills; whether she has the potential to take on roles and responsibilities that aren't directly related to her area of expertise. To answer this question, pose the following hypothetical situation to your team:

> Assume that the person being assessed declared that she didn't find her job and her area of expertise stimulating anymore and wanted some new challenges. How would this person do in a nontechnical position? Does she seem sufficiently adaptable that she could take on a new task and exhibit the same expertise in it as in her traditional area of strength?

A word of warning: Your team may overvalue an irreplaceable pro, believing that his expertise is automatically transferable to other areas—that is, if he is good at one thing, he will be sufficiently versatile to be good at something else. Unfortunately, it doesn't always work this way. As valuable as an individual is in a given area, you need to force yourself to be objective when considering his versatility potential.

Well-Placed Individuals

Like irreplaceable pros, these people are good at what they do but are not likely to move beyond the boundaries of their current jobs. They will provide stability as a change initiative is enacted, but they aren't likely to adapt quickly and easily to new assignments or ones with additional tasks. While a development program might help them become more versatile, it will be a time-intensive effort.

As opposed to the irreplaceable pro, the well-placed individual embodies a difficult-to-replace competence. In other words, this person is one notch down on the expertise scale. When your team is assessing employees as well-placed, be aware of a trait that often manifests itself:

> When change is demanded, well-placed individuals often stick with "what was" instead of growing and acquiring skills for "what will be." This lack of versatility may surface when they're asked to adjust and adapt during periods of change.

Minimally Versatile Individuals

This category is for the rigid traditionalists and narrow thinkers. The team often recognizes these people quickly because they've established reputations for doing one thing one way. Well-placed individuals won't be change leaders, but they often have contributed as participants, demonstrating the moderate flexibility necessary to learn new skills or adapt to new environments within the parameters of their position.

Minimally versatile people, on the other hand, can have a counterproductive impact on change. Perhaps the biggest red flag that can come up in an assessment meeting is when a minimally versatile individual occupies a pivotal position (or is being seriously considered for one). If this happens, the team needs to take immediate action—anything from transferring this person to a position where he'll do the change no harm or speeding his exit from the organization. Here are some tips for identifying minimally versatile people:

▲ *They often are blocked responders.* If you rate individuals as blocked, it's quite possible that they are also minimally versatile. This double whammy should start alarm bells ringing in your meeting.

▲ *They have a history of consistent inflexibility.* In your meeting, search for a pattern of rigidity. Did John react poorly when he was asked to manage a cross-functional team? Did he stubbornly refuse to use the new software? Has he rebelled whenever he was asked to work for a woman?

▲ *They are easily misidentified as well-placed.* No one likes to admit that a direct report is minimally versatile and have to tackle the subsequent actions that must be taken. I've seen teams giving highly rigid people the benefit of the doubt simply to avoid conferring this negative label. This is a dangerous practice. To guard against it, challenge a team member's assertion that someone is well-placed if you truly believe he is minimally versatile.

Figure 2-2 provides a summary of versatility categories.

Interpreting Personal Change Capacity Results

After you've rated your people for change response and versatility, you can immediately make some good guesses about change capability. When you have an individual with very high or very low change-response and versatility scores, you know he is going to either play a key role or no role in making a given change happen. When your ratings are in the middle (i.e., someone with a passive responder and limited versatility/irreplaceable pro designation), then you know you've iden-

Figure 2-2. Versatility

Future: Can the individual play a larger role, or be successful in a more complex and ambiguous job? Speculating, what is our best thinking about the individual at this point?

Most Versatile

☐ Clearly Versatile: Ready right now to play a larger, broader, or expanded role. The individual is seen as a real talent who's flexible to meet future demands of our change effort.

☐ Expandable/Versatile: Clearly capable to step up and play an expanded role in a new or more challenging setting. The issue is timing—the person is not ready now but is expandable in the future (i.e., in one to three years).

Limited Versatility

☐ Irreplaceable Pro: Technically a highly valued resource whose departure would be a significant loss. A load-bearing wall in the organization, but someone who should not take a larger or more complex task at this time.

☐ Well-Placed: At this time, the individual does a solid job, but the versatility to stretch and handle more complex tasks right now is questioned.

Minimal Versatility

☐ Minimally Versatile: Very limited capacity to handle minimal changes in routine beyond where the person is today. Will have trouble with new, diverse, and complex tasks that we might move into.

---

tified people who can provide some support but probably not much leadership, and that development probably is important before you give them anything new or challenging to do.

In addition, you need to refine your personal change capacity assessment so that it becomes actionable. This means assigning a letter grade to those being assessed based on their combined change response and versatility rating. And it means factoring in the five traits of the previous chapter—targeted skills, pivotal positions, towering strengths, development needs, and challenges/unanswered questions—so that you have a better sense of all the external factors impacting an individual's ability to lead and support change.

The way to refine your assessment is through profiling, a technique you'll find useful in "visualizing" personal change capacity.

3

Creating Profiles

At this point, you and your team have gathered information that provides you with insights about seven different factors— five primarily extrinsic factors (Chapter 1) and two key intrinsic measures (Chapter 2)—that impact the personal change capacity of various individuals. But if you are like most people embarking on this assessment process for the first time, you may be a bit confused by all the data you've accumulated.

Profiling will diminish or eliminate this confusion. As you'll see, the profile charts presented in this chapter will give you tools to organize your data and put it in usable form. Although there are certainly more profile possibilities than the six discussed here, these are common ones and they represent a wide range of personal change capacities.

The profile forms (Figures 3-1 through 3-6) contain spaces for you to record your team's decisions about change response, versatility, development needs, challenges/unanswered questions, and towering strengths, as well as input general comments. At this point, simply keep in mind the external factors of targeted skills and pivotal positions and bring them up if they seem relevant (as in the profile of Ann Screen in Figure 3-6). You'll need to pay more attention to these two factors during the final steps—analyzing weak links and defining the roadmap—of the assessment process.

In the profiling step, your objective is to become astute about interpreting the data. Before you can divide your key people into A-, B-, C-, and D-players and assess your group's change capacity, you need to become savvy about identifying the change capacity of each individual. Being savvy means first looking at the two key measures (change response and versatility ratings) and then leavening these ratings with the three internal factors (towering strength, development needs, and unanswered questions). While change response and versatility carry the most weight in your assessment, you need to be attuned to the other issues. In the general comments space of the profile charts, you'll have an opportunity to note your observations about an individual's change capacity in case there's something that a quick look at the ratings doesn't reveal. For instance, it may be that Marcia's towering strength is so crucial to your group's and the organization's change strategy that you want to devote all your resources to improving her versatility and change responsiveness quickly. Or, if you are a human resources representative on the team, you may possess additional information about a given individual that's relevant and can be included in the general comments section.

Keep these issues in mind as you consider the following six profiles.

Common Profile Types

Sharon Star

Sharon's change response/versatility rating is quite high. She's an active responder and clearly versatile. When you find someone who has this type of rating, you know you have an individual who is a likely candidate for a major role in the change process. If you need a manager to lead a change program or take on an expanded role in an organization that's moving in a new direction, this rating suggests that the person can handle the job.

Still, it is important to look at the other profile factors, beginning with towering strengths. Sharon has a terrific balance of leadership and strategic execution skills. This dovetails nicely with the business challenge Sharon's organization currently faces—it is embarking on an ambitious expansion strategy and needs people who not only can conceptualize and

Figure 3-1. Personal Change Profile #1: Sharon Star

Confidential

Name: Sharon Star   Service: 8 (yrs)

Location: Los Angeles, CA   Title: VP, Supply Chain

Change Response:
Active

Reports to: Amy Bishop   Division: _____

Years in Job: **1.5**   Position Code: _____

Versatility:
Clearly Versatile

Significant Towering Strengths	Key Development Needs
▲ Strategic Thinking —Sees patterns —Looks for opportunities and continuous improvement	▲ Sizing Up People —Needs more accuracy and to be more cautious with early read
▲ Execution Skills —Has track record of results in tough situations —Delivers results on a timely basis	▲ Strategic Agility —Can overdo her strength —Needs to be more patient with tactical or less competent people
▲ Leadership Skills —Attracts talent —Solid in her development of people	

Key Questions/Challenges

▲ Can Sharon provide leadership in a turnaround situation? She has not been involved in this situation, to date, but with the planned acquisitions downstream, this skill will be important. She needs to be tested here.

▲ Can Sharon quickly produce strong results with the new aggressive program that ties supply chain to the sales and marketing effort in the Seattle area?

▲ Can Sharon move up quickly without development? The organization doesn't need to put a talent like this at risk.

Comments

Make sure that we keep the three unanswered questions in the forefront. If we do move her up quickly, we need to ensure that she has a solid, experienced coach to work with her. She is very marketable, and while she's pleased with her job right now, we need to aggressively manage her compensation. She merits discussion every three months and needs to be given visibility.

plan where the company should be going, but can implement the plan as well.

It's instructive that the team has identified two development needs for Sharon. When someone rates this high, teams often overlook these needs, assuming that the individual's towering strengths and change response/versatility scores will compensate for any weakness. This isn't always true. In fact, Sharon needs to learn to size up people better because as the company expands, she's going to be responsible for significant hiring and promotion decisions.

The other development need—strategic agility—is also going to be important in light of the organization's direction. When you are evaluating people, keep in mind that their needs are often the flip side of their strengths. In Sharon's case, her strong strategic skills often prevent her from realizing that not everyone thinks the way she does. In the team meetings, one member noted that Sharon often grew impatient with Lee—a highly tactical thinker—because he had overlooked strategic implications when he made a recommendation to her. Rather than helping him think more strategically, she'd just criticize him for what he had missed (and do so in a curt manner).

These needs aren't critical, but they should be addressed either before Sharon is given increased responsibilities or while she is learning them—coaching might be appropriate.

There are three unanswered questions and challenges to consider related to Sharon Star's personal change capacity:

1. *Can Sharon provide leadership in a turnaround situation?* This question must be answered quickly, since part of the expansion strategy includes acquisition of a company that has been struggling. While Sharon's high change-response and versatility scores suggest that she'll do fine with a turnaround, she has no experience in this area. It might be wise to test her in some way before handing this project to her—it would be good to know in advance if her personal change capacity is compromised in any way when she's asked to deal with a company in trouble.

2. *Can Sharon produce fast sales results with the new program that ties supply chain to sales and marketing?* This

issue must also be addressed in the near future. If Sharon is lacking the requisite knowledge about the supply chain/marketing/sales connection, she may not pursue this new program as aggressively as is necessary. Some people balk at change just because it involves an area with which they are unfamiliar. Therefore, it might be wise to assess Sharon's knowledge in this area and provide her with some training if she comes up short.

3. *Can Sharon move up quickly without development?* This a tricky one. Realistically, Sharon is probably going to expect increased responsibility and leadership assignments, given her talent (someone else in the organization will select Sharon for such an assignment if you don't). Perhaps a better question is: Can Sharon handle the changes a new position demands—learning on the job and adapting as she goes along? Given all of Sharon's strengths, it seems likely she will be able to handle it. If there's any development work that should be done, the turnaround issue is probably key and you may want to focus efforts there.

As her name suggests, Sharon is a star—and not just in the performance sense of the term. Not only are her change response and versatility ratings high, but her towering strengths match the organization's targeted skills. If anything should be noted in the general comments section of the profile, it is that stars are highly marketable commodities and that Sharon's compensation requirements should be met to ensure she doesn't leave the company for a better offer. As long as this issue is addressed, Sharon's personal change capacity is high and she should be given a wide range of new roles and responsibilities.

George Grown

While George didn't score quite as well as Sharon, his change response/versatility rating is still high. His passive change-response rating indicates that he sometimes hasn't been as eager to lead change as he might have been, yet he's close enough to an active responder rating that he should be considered for a position that is pivotal to your group's transformation. His clearly versatile rating means that George probably could take on an expanded role in a changing company within the year.

George's mix of towering strengths and development needs suggests someone who may be a little gun-shy in the face of major change. While he certainly is skilled at project management, relationship building, and other leadership tasks, he is not someone who is facile at creating a strategic vision for a new division or who will seize opportunities by spotting emerging trends. His slight overreliance on tried-and-true methods also means that he may resist new approaches in a changing, chaotic environment.

None of these factors is fatal. Based on his strengths and ratings, George may only need some mentoring from a skilled strategist and innovative thinker. With a bit of help and time, George can grow into the role of change leader and perform admirably.

The big unanswered questions concerning George are whether he'll be able to handle more innovative thinking and multiple projects—skills required for the change-based programs that George could be involved in. When you reach the individual development phase, different options to help George with these issues should be discussed.

As you review each individual profile with your team, you'll probably come up with a number of ideas to help an individual enhance his personal change capacity. This is fine, even though the individual development phase of this process is yet to come. Make notes now for what needs to be done later. With someone such as George, who is on the cusp of being a change leader—whose change response/versatility ratings are high and whose development needs are low (relatively speaking)—you should plan on giving individual feedback. This profile type is eager to grow, and if you reward and recognize his strengths, he'll be that much more willing to take risks and work on his strategic skills.

One of the mistakes you can easily make with someone such as George is to decide that "he's close enough" and that there's no immediate need for any development. While George comes close to meeting your needs, he's not close enough to

Figure 3-2. Personal Change Profile #2: George Grown

Confidential

Name: George Grown   Service: 6 (yrs)

Location: Greensburg, PA   Title: Senior Manager

Reports to: Tom DeBarr   Division: _____

Years in Job: 1   Position Code: _____

Change Response:
Passive

Versatility:
Expandable

Significant Towering Strengths	Key Development Needs
▲ Project Management Skills —Solid planning —Negotiation skills —Seeks feedback	▲ Strategic Thinking —Looks into the future, crafting and shaping a compelling vision
▲ Team Leadership —Quickly finds common ground —"Early knower" (gets informal and solid information in time to do something early)	▲ Getting on board with change that is different from what he has developed (uses "tried and true" a little more than he should)
▲ Hungry —Wants to learn and grow/personally —Ambitious in the most positive light	▲ Idea Sharing —Has good ideas but should bring those forward in senior management meetings more
▲ Respected across the board	

Key Questions/Challenges

▲ Can/will George develop more innovative thinking that takes him beyond the immediate projects that he handles?

▲ Can George step up to managing multiple projects (e.g., Launch of Tech 102 marketing entry)? He could make a large contribution here if he focuses on this.

Comments

A development plan needs to be put together and implemented soon that gets George more in a strategic framework. He has many solid strengths and is a key player, but needs to become more strategically agile. Work in strategy should round him out nicely.

deliver if you have a change project that calls upon the skills he lacks. His change response score suggests that he may pull back when asked to take any risks in a changing environment, and that's the last thing you want to happen.

When evaluating George's change capacity, recognize that he is somewhat flawed in a key area (strategic skills) and has a history of not responding with leadership and drive in areas that demand use of these skills. This is a point to consider when deciding if George is an A-player or B-player. If there isn't time for him to develop the proper skills, or if a change strategy puts him in a position where he needs to use these skills, you may want to keep him out of a pivotal position.

Sam Solid

When you have a profile like Sam's, you may feel disappointed initially. His passive change response and moderate versatility scores are below present and future stars such as Sharon and George. At the same time, his personal change capacity is still decent. Because of his towering technical strengths and his ability to nurture talent, he may be instrumental in helping you carry out a change effort. No one needs all change leaders and no change followers. In fact, Sam will probably be a critical piece of the puzzle as the company and your group evolves. As an irreplaceable pro, he'll give you the expertise and stability you need behind you to take risks and try new approaches. Sam's gift for finding and growing talent also is significant. Whenever you find a technically skilled person who can also bring out the best in people, you have someone who will contribute to change efforts in a variety of ways (including helping bring along others who may become change leaders).

Sam is low-maintenance; he'll accept new initiatives and processes with equanimity. People who profile like Sam usually have a weakness or two—in Sam's case it is difficulty presenting to senior management—but this shouldn't be a cause of great concern. Sam is a sixteen-year veteran of the company whom you know you can depend on to support

Figure 3-3. Personal Change Profile #3: Sam Solid

Confidential

Name: Sam Solid   Service: 16 (yrs)

Location: Grafton, WV   Title: Director, Tech
                                   Support

Reports to: Pat Kalbaugh   Division: _____

Years in Job: 4   Position Code: _____

Change Response:
Passive

Versatility:
Irreplaceable Pro

Significant Towering Strengths	Key Development Needs
▲ Technical Management —Produces results consistently/ little fanfare	▲ Strategic Thinking
▲ Builds Talent —Has track record of seeing talent throughout company	▲ Presentation Skills —Seems to freeze up, especially in front of senior managers
▲ Technical Scanning —Looks for ideas inside and outside for continuous improvement	▲ Peer Negotiation Skills —Needs to reach out more

Key Questions/Challenges

▲ Can/will Sam improve his presence, comfort level, and presentation skills in front of senior management? Additionally, because of his technical strength, he could be a significant asset in front of customers.

▲ Will Sam reach out to his peers more on a regular basis? If called to his attention he will do it, but he needs to be more dedicated to this development need. Was critical with the project involving our new joint technical agreement with Boeing.

Comments

Let's make sure that Sam does not drop off the radar screen as we implement the new changes. He needs more visibility—any time this has happened, Sam has risen to the occasion. Let's see if we can get Sam on the new product introduction process—he has much to add, and it would get him out beyond his technical comfort zone.

change leaders' efforts. While there may be some other nagging questions about Sam, they aren't make-or-break ones.

When you come across a profile like Sam's, be careful not to take the person for granted. Whereas someone like Sharon might pull your group in the direction of change, she'll pull everyone on Sam's back. It's easy to neglect the Sam Solids of the world and assume they'll always be there and do a good job, no matter what changes are coming down. In fact, irreplaceable pros like Sam have needs, and if you don't meet them, he may leave and find another company that will.

At Baxter International, we had one of the world's premier plastics engineers, an irreplaceable pro like Sam. It turned out that this engineer had quietly been requesting a larger space to work, and he'd been ignored. Finally, his boss came to me and said, "Look, this guy is a genius at what he does and you're telling me you can't give him a larger space? I'll tell you what I'm going to do; I'm going to give him my office, because if he's not happy and doing what he does best, both you and I won't be around because we wasted this incredibly valuable asset."

The engineer received a larger office, thanks to his boss, who recognized the importance of irreplaceable pros to the process of change.

If you find one of your people fits this profile type, you want to keep him on a growth track. The Sam Solids of the world sometimes slip into comfort zones; while everything around them is changing, they continue doing as they've always done. No matter what type of development program you plan for Sam, he's probably never going to have the personal change capacity of someone like Sharon. On the other hand, Sam will respond positively to change and take on a broader role within his technical area of expertise. If you push him in the direction of acquiring new knowledge and testing new approaches within this well-defined area, Sam will contribute fresh ideas to a change program and still lend solid support.

It's wise to note in the general comments section that Sam's versatility is linked to his area of expertise. Outside of that area, Sam will have a lower change capacity.

Terry Tech

Like Sam, Terry has good technical skills. Unlike Sam, his change response and versatility ratings suggest someone who is going to have problems during times of change—especially in terms of managing and leading others. Terry is the classic profile of someone who has been promoted beyond his level of competence; he's been moved up because of his technical skill rather than his ability to lead, work with others, and come up with innovative ideas. If the changes going on in your group involve more teamwork, managing by consensus, or developing talent, Terry is going to disappoint you. As a reactive change responder and with a well-placed versatility rating, Terry is limited in how much he can contribute as your group evolves.

This doesn't mean that he won't contribute. As you can see from Terry's towering strengths, he works hard, possesses important skills, and will try to make things happen single-handedly. In the old business paradigm of command-and-control leadership and pyramid structure, Terry was fine. In changing environments, however, this profile type has significant problems. The odds are you have a lot of people like Terry in your organization.

The overarching unanswered questions you need to ask are: Can Terry make the transition to a new and expanded mode of work? If he is called on to lead or manage—not just do things—can he handle it? If he's given the new responsibility of nurturing the talent brought into the company, will he demonstrate the patience and flexibility required to work with a diverse group of people?

You have a number of options for this type of profile. You want to retain Terry's expertise, but you also need to be wary of his lower-middle personal change capacity. Transferring Terry to a role more suited to this capacity might be appropriate. If the structure of your group and company changes, Terry may have great difficulty reporting to someone who expects him to lead and manage in a way that's beyond his current capacity. Finding a role that allows Terry to do what he

Figure 3-4. Personal Change Profile #4: Terry Tech

Confidential

Name: Terry Tech	Service: 10 (yrs)	**Change Response:** Reactive
Location: Charleston, WV	Title: _____	
Reports to: Bill Morgan	Division: _____	**Versatility:** Well Placed
Years in Job: 3	Position Code: _____	

Significant Towering Strengths	Key Development Needs
▲ Technical Strength (world class)	▲ Runs over people to deliver; "takes no prisoners"
▲ Personal Commitment —Works very hard to make it happen	
▲ Has personally pulled a number of key projects out of the fire at the last minute	▲ Frame of reference for success locked in by "what was"; has not stepped up to the change agenda
	▲ Gives up too easily on people (not good at developing talent)
	▲ Team Play —Has a history of poor relationships and flare-ups across the organization

Key Questions/Challenges

▲ Can Terry learn to manage and lead instead of being the chief expert? His skill is not questioned, but with the large Intel coproject (which he wants to lead) at hand, this cold spell disaster.

▲ Can Terry utilize his know-how and translate it to the talent that we are bringing into the organization? He gives up too quickly on those that don't respond to his particular style right away—our engineers do not want to work in his unit.

Comments

We need to get Terry on a project that tests whether he can develop beyond his technical area. The new ADC Communications project, where he could colead and assist Bernie Fout, one of the best project managers we have, should be looked at. If he cannot demonstrate that he can prosper under those conditions, then we most likely need to look at an individual contributor technical role.

does best—and removing him from most management and leadership responsibilities—may be necessary.

It's also possible that Terry can be developed so that he can assume a larger role in your changing group. Technically talented people such as Terry often are eager to foster changes and implement innovations within their area of expertise. Capitalize on Terry's inherent motivation to learn and grow in his area, and give him the chance to develop new skills and knowledge that he can put to use for the organization.

While Terry's change capacity isn't high, it can fluctuate a bit, depending on how he's developed and what role he's asked to play in a changing environment. In general comments, you should underscore the unanswered questions about Terry. Do you need him to lead or manage implementation of change, or do you simply need him to provide technical support? Keep this question in mind when you determine if Terry is a B-player or a C-player.

Bill Brightplus

Bill represents a conundrum. He possesses the brainpower necessary to handle just about any new assignment, no matter how challenging it might be. At the same time, he has a track record of responding to unfamiliar people and situations in negative ways. His change response/versatility rating illustrates this conundrum. As a seriously reactive change responder, Bill has a history of getting himself in scrapes whenever he has to deal with new people; he's blown up at supervisors who have tried to give feedback designed to help him master a new process or procedure. Yet in terms of versatility, he's in the expandable category. The team recognizes that Bill has the cognitive ability to take on many of the new assignments that will be part and parcel of the division's new structure.

This profile type is relatively easy to spot. These people often went to top business schools and were heavily recruited. In their first few years on the job, they were viewed as stars, and their skills package placed them on the fast track, earning them promotions and choice assignments. As individual con-

Figure 3-5. Personal Change Profile #5: Bill Brightplus

Confidential

Name: Bill Brightplus   Service: 6 (yrs)

Location: Washington, DC   Title: Manager,
                                  Financial
                                  Strategy

Reports to: Mitch Reagan   Division: _____

Years in Job: 2   Position Code: _____

Change Response:
Reactive

Versatility:
Expandable

Significant Towering Strengths	Key Development Needs
▲ Bright + + +	▲ People Skills —Impatient —Can come across as arrogant
▲ Analytic Skills —Market analysis —Strategic thinking; played key role in setting up our strategy-planning process	▲ Likes his way; ignores input
	▲ Feedback —Has trouble accepting —Takes a great deal of energy to manage him and the various skirmishes that he gets into
	▲ Peer Relationships —Has composure issues —Can't seem to find common ground —Too rigid

Key Questions/Challenges

▲ No question of Bill's intellectual horsepower; however, can he significantly improve his people skills? The company is getting fatigued by his behavior.

▲ Can/will Bill learn to learn? He needs to be open to feedback and has not demonstrated willingness so far; this needs to change.

Comments

Bill is very talented, but needs to improve his approach with people. A coaching program with Gordon Martin might be appropriate. All of those individuals involved with him know what he can do. We also might look for the best project—a safe arena where he can be coached and make progress. Need to monitor the situation—we could lose this talent. It would do him no good to leave this company for a larger job outside.

tributors, they did well. But after a while, their flaws surfaced. In Bill's case, the flaws manifested themselves as arrogance, stubbornness, and poor peer relationships. These flaws often surfaced when Bill was asked to use emotional rather than cognitive intelligence. When he was asked to actively listen to another person, to motivate, or to absorb feedback, he responded in negative ways.

People like Bill become stuck in the pattern of the shooting star: They shine brightly at first, then burn out quickly because of their flaws. I've seen people repeat this pattern in organization after organization, job assignment after job assignment. Many times, they don't even realize they are stuck in this pattern and assume they simply have to work harder to avoid flaming out. In fact, they just end up flaming out with more gusto.

Don't assign this profile type a major change role that requires anything more than cognitive competencies. If you need this person to handle a new or expanded assignment, you must first have a "get real" conversation with him. In other words, you need to confront him with his pattern and work with him to break it. Good coaching may be a necessary development path to pursue.

Bill's change capacity is barely average, but mitigating factors, such as significant development needs and towering strengths that probably don't dovetail with your group's change goals, may send this rating plummeting. On the other hand, if you just need Bill's brainpower to drive a given change, his change capacity may be better than it seems at first glance. All this should be summarized in the comments section.

Ann Screen

When you find someone who has a low change-response/versatility rating like Ann, the first question you need to address is: Does she currently occupy a pivotal position or is she being considered for a pivotal position? If Ann is pivotal to the change being contemplated, you're in trouble.

Not only is she a blocked change responder, but she's

Figure 3-6. Personal Change Profile #6: Ann Screen

Confidential

Name: Ann Screen   Service: 14 (yrs)

Location: Athens, GA   Title: Sales Manager

Reports to: Patrick Duffy   Division: _____

Years in Job: 8   Position Code: _____

Change Response: Blocked

Versatility: Minimally Versatile

Significant Towering Strengths	Key Development Needs
▲ Knows Customer Base —Customers like her —Has established long-standing relationships	▲ Producing Results on a Timely Basis —Has not grown the region that has potential
	▲ Teamwork —Pays little attention to peer relationships —Feels as if unit is stand alone
	▲ Composure —Has lost her cool at meetings —Has turned off some customers —"Prickly"
	▲ Flexibility —Feels that her way is the only way —Not approachable for input

Key Questions/Challenges
▲ Can Ann quickly improve her results? She requires cross-selling and lateral coordination—areas that she has refused to work on. Talks this to boss, but nothing happens.
▲ Can/will Ann improve her people-handling skills? She has a reputation of running over a number of people.
▲ Ann is protective of her customer base, which she has had for a number of years. Does her rather "prickly" nature affect us in the marketplace? Does this play a role in the marginal growth in a seemingly hot area?

Comments
No doubt that Ann is respected by some customers. It is getting her beyond her comfort zone that is the challenge. Overall, this issue needs to be resolved rather quickly, but she has to want it also.

minimally versatile. Typically, individuals like Ann self-destruct at the first whiff of change, or they sabotage the change process. They respond in all sorts of negative ways to anything new or different, and they are unable to handle expanded roles and responsibilities.

As you can see from the profile, Ann has a redeeming quality that has kept her employed. She's good with customers. Like many salespeople who have been in their jobs for a significant period of time, Ann has settled into a groove and coasted; she's unwilling to approach new markets or restructure current customer relationships in more effective ways. Ann is protected by the fact that she brings in business, customers like her, and she has a lot of valuable information in her head about her customers. Though there are annual discussions about "what to do about Ann," no action is ever taken because her customer knowledge makes her just valuable enough to keep in place.

On the other hand, everyone wishes there was something they could do about her. It's not just that she has failed to grow her region. Ann is closed off to new ideas and new relationships. Her development needs are significant and numerous. Coaching, training, and mentoring all would be useful to her.

Given Ann's profile, it would take at least three or four years to develop her in ways that would meet change goals, and you need her ready to go within the year. Considering the direction and speed with which the CEO is taking the company, development may not be an option for Ann. One of the challenges/unanswered questions for Ann is cross-selling and lateral coordination. In the past, she has put up great resistance to both of these goals. In the near future, every sales manager will be required to pursue these goals vigorously.

Perhaps Ann can be moved out of harm's way (and change's way) and given a less demanding role. It may also be necessary to ask her to leave the organization altogether. Her low ratings in terms of both versatility and change response make her towering strength irrelevant to the discussion. The only thing to keep in mind is that people do change given the right development program and experiences, and over an extended period of time, it is possible that Ann's change capacity might improve.

Profiling Is an Art, Not a Science

The objective of your team isn't to create the definitive portrait of a key person as much as it is to create a holistic picture. Your team needs to engage in a discussion around the issues highlighted in the individual profiles of your key people. You must consider not only each individual's crucial change response and versatility ratings, but how the other factors temper that rating. A looming unanswered question or a crucial towering strength (that's absent or in abundance) has to be examined. While your team doesn't have to make development decisions on the spot or project exactly what roles and responsibilities someone can handle in the future, you should weigh the possibilities. Even though you can be pretty sure that Sharon Star will be an A-player under most circumstances and Ann Screen will be a D-player, it is good to weigh the factors that might affect how they'll perform as your group embarks on its change path.

In the case of the four other people and their profile types, their status is a bit more uncertain. While their change response and versatility ratings suggest a specific grade, you need to create these profiles and discuss them, in confidence, with your team in order to obtain a reading of who your A-, B-, C-, and D-players are.

Ultimately, it will do you little good to know that one person is an A-player and another is a C-player. What is much more useful is knowing the total breakout of A's, B's, C's, and D's in your group. Determining this group change capacity is our next step.

4

Identifying Group Change Capacity

Determining whether your people are A-, B-, C-, or D-players is a relatively easy task at this point. You simply need to look at their change response and versatility ratings and plot where they fit on the matrix shown in Figure 4-1 of this chapter. But what you see might not be what you get. As I've emphasized in earlier chapters, other factors may influence these grades, so it is important to understand when and how to adjust an individual's grade.

Again, the individual grade isn't designed as a performance rating and shouldn't be used as such. Branding someone as a C-player is wrong for many reasons, not the least of which is that a highly skilled person might be a C-player and, upon learning this grade, might be offended and become less effective (or even leave the organization). The real use of these letter grades is as a shorthand to help you assess group change capacity. The sum of the grades of your key players tells you whether you are ready to implement your piece of a change strategy. Do you have all A-players or all D-players? Do you have a nice mix of A's, B's, and C's, or is everyone clustered in the B and C groups? It may be that you need to develop your people over the course of a year before you are ready to drive change.

It is also possible that you are going to need outside help and have to move people around internally. You may have intrinsically high change capacity among your employees but lack the towering strengths that match up with the targeted skills crucial for change. Human resources (HR) professionals are very useful at helping make these determinations. Most HR people are experienced in the development and recruiting issues that often take center stage at this point, and they can answer such questions as how long it might take to develop C-players into B-players, or how likely it is that your group can afford or even find the A-player that it is missing.

HR can facilitate analyzing where your group stands relative to the change that is required, a process that is detailed next.

Putting Your People in the Right Place

The group/team change capacity matrix (see Figure 4-1) is a tool that allows you to form a composite picture of where your people stand. As an illustration, each of the six individuals profiled in Chapter 3 have been placed in a box. The matrix has twenty boxes, so there are potentially twenty different personal change capacity types.

As you look at the boxes within the overall matrix, you can derive a sense of how much talent you possess (or lack) to drive change. Now let's overlay a "grading scale" (see Figure 4-2) so you can see which boxes correspond to which letter grades.

The big question is: When should your team adjust these intrinsic grades? To a certain extent, you need to be careful about adjusting them. The combination of change response and versatility is a powerful measure of change capacity, and you don't want to downgrade an A-player to a B-player just because his towering strength doesn't perfectly match a targeted skill or because there's an unanswered question that bothers you a bit. In other words, there needs to be a sufficiently compelling reason to change a grade.

When to Change an Individual's Grade

1. *The change strategy demands a skill that is an individual's Achilles' heel.* For instance, Jack is rated as a passive

Figure 4-1. Group/Team Change Capacity Matrix

VERSATILITY

	(MV) Minimally Versatile	(WP) Well-Placed	(IP) Irreplaceable Pro	(E) Expandable	(C) Clearly Versatile
Active					▲ Sharon Star
Passive			▲ Sam Solid	▲ George Grown	
Reactive		▲ Terry Tech		▲ Bill Brightplus	
Blocked	▲ Ann Screen				

C H A N G E   R E S P O N S E

Figure 4-2. Overall Management Depth

VERSATILITY

CHANGE RESPONSE	(MV) Minimally Versatile	(WP) Well-Placed	(IP) Irreplaceable Pro	(E) Expandable	(C) Clearly Versatile
Active	✕				▲ Sharon Star
Passive		"B" Players	▲ Sam Solid	▲ George Crown "A" Players	
Reactive		▲ Terry Tech "C" Players		▲ Bill Brightplus	
Blocked	▲ Ann Screen "D" Players			✕	✕

A Players——Should get positions/aggressively manage them
B Players——Stay in place and develop/must stay up as bar is raised
C Players——Must improve quickly/aggressive approach to improve change capability is required
D Players——Questionable/performance improvement plan that's monitored or action required

change responder and expandable/versatile, making him a B-player. As a B-player, Jack should be considered for a significant role in the change effort. It's likely that he can handle new responsibilities of greater scope and scale; he might even be able to occupy a pivotal position in time, given the proper development. But when the evaluation team meets, one team member points out that her group is being asked to conduct a search internally and externally for people to head up a new, state-of-the-art manufacturing plant. Though Jack is a highly skilled engineer, this team member explains, he has made singularly poor hiring decisions in the past and tends to play favorites when it comes to promotions. In this instance, it makes sense to downgrade Jack from a B player to a C-player, reserving the right to upgrade him in another change-based scenario. Because HR people are often privy to detailed information about an individual's competencies and performance weaknesses, they usually provide valuable advice about this potentially grade-changing subject.

2. *A major development need can't be met on a timely basis or requires a major shift in attitude and behavior.* Development can't work miracles, and if you are counting on one to turn a follower into a leader in a matter of weeks or to transform someone's personality, then you're making a mistake. Change often requires people to acquire new skills or exhibit new attitudes and behaviors, and it may be impossible for them to do so within your time frame. If this is the case, an A-player may not perform like an A-player. You may want to assign someone a temporarily lower grade and upgrade them only when there's evidence that they've acquired the targeted skills or behaviors. Leadership skills can take years to develop. On the other hand, presentation skills can often be developed after only a few weeks of intensive training. If someone on your team is involved in training and development, he'll be able to give you a sense if a development objective is feasible given your time constraints.

3. *Change response and versatility ratings generally don't reflect change response and versatility ratings in an area of towering strength.* I've found that C-players, especially, can be

underrated. Well-placed and irreplaceable pros (in terms of versatility ratings) and reactive or even blocked change responders often demonstrate an anomalous ratings spike when it comes to their area of expertise. I recall an IT manager who was rigid and resistant to most types of change, yet he underwent a Jekyll and Hyde metamorphosis when he was dealing with information systems. This manager demonstrated outright hostility to other managers when he was placed on a cross-functional team and refused to push decision making down to lower levels as mandated by the new CEO, yet he was a leader for change in his department. Demonstrating daring, initiative, and innovation, he single-handedly pushed for a new system that was costly and involved radically different software that would require extensive training. Nonetheless, he was adamant that the long-term gains more than outweighed the short-term headaches, and he took a big risk in pushing for and leading the implementation of the new system (a risk that paid off in the long run). In this type of situation—when your change pivots on the specific towering strength a low-rated individual possesses—it makes sense to adjust the grade upward.

4. *An unanswered question or unmet challenge looms large enough that you don't want to take the chance of overrating an individual, especially someone targeted for a pivotal position.* A compelling unanswered question is whether someone has the motivation or ambition to become a true change leader. A significant unmet challenge involves overcoming a weakness, such as being able to manage diversity or work in a team environment. As high as someone's change response and versatility ratings might be, if there is a big question mark next to her name, it makes her ability to lead and support change suspect. Sometimes the questions are minor and insufficent to affect a grade; for example, a tendency to show up late for work and meetings probably shouldn't have an impact on personal change capacity. Neither should unfounded rumors or unsubstantiated accusations. You need to be careful not to let gossip and innuendo influence your team's assessment. It is only when you are fairly certain that a question or challenge

is real and significant and that a pivotal position is involved that your team should reevaluate a grade.

Helping Your Team Make Tough Decisions

At times, your team will need to use common sense to supplement the matrix and other tools provided in this chapter. While you need to be careful about letting team members voice subjective opinions about individuals—they'll tend to overrate, especially in cultures of accommodation—a bit of discussion can sometimes determine what grade an individual really deserves.

To foster an intelligent discussion, review the following descriptions of each type of letter rating:

▲ *A-talent.* These people can play major roles in leading and managing just about any type of change. You can give them new and expanded responsibilities, and their change capacity is sufficiently high that they can adapt with relative ease.

▲ *B-talent.* This group consists of individuals who will perform well in the midst of change. Although you can't always count on them to drive the change, you can depend on them for support and performance. It's also likely that this group can handle new roles and responsibilities, given sufficient time and development.

▲ *C-talent.* These people probably won't add value during periods of change. Given the combination of their change response and versatility scores, they will only make marginal contributions (if that). Be aware that C-players come in all shapes and sizes (and in various combinations of change response and versatility ratings).

▲ *D-talent.* These individuals have demonstrated negative responses to change in the past and it is doubtful they will be able to handle unfamiliar or "stretch" assignments in the future. In fact, as the organization performance bar is raised, they probably won't be able to clear the new height. While you may try to assist them, the odds are that they don't have much of a future in the company.

While it's true that development can move people up in grade, it's also true that this type of development usually takes time. If you don't have much time to spare, then don't give someone the benefit of the doubt and fool yourself. Don't let a team member sway everyone with a passionate argument about how "Sam just needs a bit of coaching to push him into B-territory," or "Judy's one of our rising stars, and we'd be making a mistake if we didn't make her an A-player."

Ultimately, you need to keep the team focused on the data you've accumulated—specifically:

▲ The change response and versatility ratings
▲ The three key internal factors—towering strengths, development needs, and challenges/unanswered questions

Let the first two measures be your grading guide and the three factors be your tiebreaker. If that doesn't work and if there is still disagreement among the team, then let the boss of the assessed individual be the decision maker (assuming this boss is part of the assessment team).

Sometimes consensus is difficult. One team member has dug in his heels on giving Judy an A-rating, a second insists she's a B-player, and a third is on the fence. To break the logjam, it sometimes helps to describe each letter category in more detail, providing team members with a better picture of what C-players look like and the change roles best suited to them, then contrasting this information with a detailed portrait of B-players and their roles. Let's discuss some perspectives on each type of talent that you might share with your team.

If you are wondering whether someone you're assessing really belongs in the A-talent group, ask the following question:

How well do they learn from their experiences?

For example, Sharon Star and George Grown, two of the profile types covered in Chapter 3 and mapped onto the matrix in Figure 4-1, have the ability to absorb lessons from both failures and triumphs.[1] They may not have implemented a new strategy or run their first cross-functional team effectively in the past, but they derived learning from these experiences that will help them handle new and changing situations better in the future. This doesn't mean that they are necessarily "best and brightest" types; it is a mistake to assume that the "brightest" are the best workers. Likewise, Bill Brightplus is not an A-player, although at times throughout his career he had been described that way.

When you look at B-talent, you find Sam Solid, the quintessential solid citizen. He is among the irreplaceable pros and the well-placed individuals, the people who don't have trouble with change (but don't usually drive it, either). Technically, these people are usually at the top of their game. The problem occurs when B-players are promoted into A-talent positions solely because of their technical expertise. In these situations, they often fall back on their expertise and manage change from a narrow perspective. Sam Solid, for instance, would never be able to come up with the sort of innovative ideas or motivational concepts necessary to move a team to the performance level dictated by a new organizational strategy, whereas someone like Sharon Star would.

The key is plugging your B-players into crucial and appropriate support roles and not overestimating their versatility based on their technical achievements (and not broadening their responsibilities in ways that are beyond them).

As you can tell, C-talent takes many forms. You can have someone like Terry Tech who is a reactive responder and is considered well-placed from a versatility standpoint. You might also find someone who is expandable in terms of versatility but is a reactive responder. And you might also encounter a manager who is a passive responder with limited versatility. All these individuals are change-flawed—that is, they will have serious shortcomings with strategy, tactics, or people when their environment shifts or when they are asked to do something new and different.

The last category—D-talent—is one that spells doom for change. You cannot overestimate the damage these individuals can do to a change effort, especially if they are in leadership or managerial positions. It's not just that their rigidity and negative response to change will make them personally ineffective. It's that they will prevent other people—peers and direct reports—from performing at peak potential. Their resistance to new directions and procedures turns people who might otherwise be very supportive into disinterested observers. Their unwillingness to take chances and expand the depth and breadth of their work prevents others from taking on new challenges as well.

As you contemplate this last category of D-players, keep the following shocking statistic in mind:

> In most organizations that are starting to use this process, I have found that 20 to 25 percent of the people assessed fall into the C- and D-talent group.

As one top executive said to me after an assessment, "If you would have asked me beforehand how many D-players we have, I would have said 5 percent. This is scary."

It is scary, but it is even more scary to underestimate the percentage of people in this group and depend on them to lead and implement a change program. Therefore, don't be afraid to identify people as D's if they really deserve this grade.

Finally, don't assign a grade because you have a stereotyped image of what an A-, B-, C-, or D-player "looks like." While certain generalizations can be made about each talent group, there is room for very different types of people in each category. Sharon Star and George Grown, for instance, are both A-players. This means you can count on both of them to do very well no matter what change challenge you place before them. At the same time, you need to be aware of their differences and development needs and how that affects their personal change capacities (see Figures 3-1 and 3-2 in Chapter 3).

The most obvious difference is their job experience. Sharon is operating as a senior executive, where the skill set is more strategic, and she has a larger job, whereas George has more of a traditional day-to-day emphasis where the strategic component is secondary. People without that much experience often are passive responders; they need more time on the job before they feel sufficiently comfortable with change to tackle a large, unfamiliar project.

Telling Patterns

Once you've decided on a final talent grade for each individual, replot the matrix in Figure 4-1 by adding the talent grades. The new matrix, shown in Figure 4-2, now presents a clear indication of your group change capacity. I've found that this matrix is an effective measure of group change capacity whether you are evaluating a small group or an entire organization. It enables you to eyeball where people cluster and get a good sense of whether you have the talent necessary to drive change—or whether you need to develop or recruit that talent if it is missing.

Clearly, if you have 50 percent or more of your people clustering in the A and B categories, you are probably in pretty good shape. If most of your employees are C-players and D-players, you're probably in trouble. Once you've done the profiles and charted the matrix, the rest of the assessment is easy. It doesn't take a genius to see the big talent picture. The sum total of the personal change capacity of your key people will be a good indication whether you are ready for the changes being planned.

Before moving on to the next issue—analyzing your weak links—let's look at four problematic patterns found on the talent matrix and what they signify:

▲ *Lots of stars.* You have a preponderance of A's and B's, and at first glance this might seem like a reason for celebration. This may be the case; you're loaded with talent and bench strength and should be able to transform the company or your

group with the greatest of ease. Beware, however, of two problems. First, your team may have overestimated your talent
base. This happens for all sorts of reasons (e.g., no one wants
to offend anyone, wishful thinking), but what you need to do
is a reality check. You might want to play devil's advocate and
ask the team to reevaluate your people or call in your boss or
another outside person for an opinion. The other, less serious
problem is that you have too many leaders and not enough
followers. Everyone wants to lead the change, but you're lacking the support group of irreplaceable pros necessary to implement new policies and processes.

▲ *Middle-of-the-road results.* In other words, your people are clustered in B and C categories. No matter what change
you have planned, you need people who will contribute great
ideas and vision and move it forward. Without A-players, you
are going to be disappointed in how people execute the change
strategy. You may need to recruit A's or develop promising B's.

▲ *C-talent galore.* It easy to rationalize a cluster of C's,
insisting that you have one strong A who will transform the
organization single-handedly or believing that you can quickly
develop C-players into B-players. The problem is not being
alarmed at all the people who have poor track records when it
comes to change or seem incapable of taking on new roles and
responsibilities. This should be a red flag if ever there was one.

▲ *Too many D-players.* While it is unlikely that all your
key people are D-players (if they are, it may be time to look for
another job), you may find that an uncomfortable number of
people fall into this talent group. Development probably isn't
the answer in this situation; it is unlikely that you have the
time, resources, patience, or ability to move these people up
to the place they need to be. What you need to look at is the
possibility of transferring some of them to nonchange positions or letting some of them go and recruiting others to take
their place. You may also have to go to your boss and explain
that you need time and resources to get your people ready to
implement your piece of the change strategy. HR may need to
become more involved from recruiting and selection angles to
replace your D-talent with A-, B-, and C-players.

I don't want to make this process sound complicated. However, by this point, you should be able to assess the following:

▲ Do you have the talent necessary to drive change?

▲ If you and your organization are coming up short, what do you have to do to obtain the talent you need (e.g., possibly a combination of development programs and new recruiting)?

The last question doesn't have to be answered just yet, but your team should at least be talking about this issue so it is ready to make decisions in the roadmap step.

Before you start creating a plan based on the group change capacity of your key people, there's an interim step: determining the change-related vulnerabilities of your group—in other words, their weak links.

5

Analyzing Weak Links

As a consultant, I sometimes refer to group change capacity as a human asset inventory: It reveals whether a group has the human assets necessary to make change happen. As you uncover these assets, certain corresponding liabilities are revealed. In terms of the measures of change response and versatility as well as the five other factors assessed, you have a good sense of where your group's strengths and weaknesses reside. However, there are other weaknesses that exist just out of range of your assessment so far. While you may quickly know if someone is missing a towering strength demanded by change or if you're overloaded with C-players and D-players, other vulnerabilities don't always show up without additional assessments.

The following are common change capacity weaknesses that can cause a crack in an otherwise sound foundation:

- ▲ Misidentifying pivotal positions
- ▲ Ignoring a lack of functional depth or positional backups
- ▲ Overlooking your vulnerability to losing key people
- ▲ Failing to factor in significant personal change idiosyncrasies

Change is a delicate mechanism, and all it takes is one overlooked part to gum up the works. This weak link analysis is designed to spot flaws that otherwise might be overlooked.

Pivotal Positions

Previously you conducted a quick analysis of your pivotal positions. Now you are armed with the additional data necessary to explore your initial assumptions in more depth. Discussions with your team to identify who is pivotal often yield insights about the positions that are equally pivotal. You may comment on Mark's low change-response score and someone will say, "Hey, wait a second, isn't Mark in a position to make or break this strategy?"

Let's start out by agreeing that anywhere from 10 percent to 20 percent of your positions will be pivotal. You may be fortunate in that the people you've already assessed occupy pivotal positions, and all of them have solid change response and versatility ratings. It is more likely, however, that some of your pivotal positions are either occupied by people you haven't assessed or managers whose personal change capacity leaves something to be desired.

Figure 5-1 is a form you can use to identify the pivotal positions in your organization, who currently occupies them, and their change response and versatility ratings.

It may seem obvious what the pivotal positions are. If you are attempting a small-scale, small-scope change, this may be

Figure 5-1. Pivotal Positions Chart

Senior Level Positions—Tier 2			
Total # Positions = _____		Total Pivotal Positions = _____	
Pivotal Position	Present Incumbent	Change Response	Versatility

true. If you simply want to install a new software system in your department, one pivotal position is certainly your IT director. But most change programs are broader and more complex than getting the bugs out of the new software. At first glance, it's not always obvious who is pivotal; you need to do some thinking and ask some questions to determine what really is going to be important strategically and tactically as you implement your strategy. Unlikely positions may turn out to be pivotal. For instance, a large organization was attempting to change its channels of distribution, and one of the pivotal positions was "relationship manager." Though the position was outside of the sales group—it had been created to help the company form alliances with competitors in order to facilitate knowledge sharing—it was at the heart of the company's strategy. The company needed to form alliances with a variety of retailers it had never worked with before, and the relationship manager had the skills and resources to open these doors.

In many instances, the simplest way to identify pivotal positions is to talk to the change leader or change agent in charge of implementing a given strategy. These people usually have a good handle on the positions they are going to lean on to help them roll out the strategy. Human resources (HR) also may have a good idea of what positions are going to be absolutely critical in a changing unit or organization. Many times, business managers have asked HR to help them identify pivotal positions for a change effort and recruit and train people accordingly. HR may be able to enlighten everyone by identifying the likely pivotal positions that impact your area.

After you identify the key positions, you simply need to fill out the pivotal position form (Figure 5-1). If you've already assessed the individuals who occupy pivotal positions, then this step is easy. If you haven't, your team needs to go back to the earlier steps and rate them according to change response and versatility. (While you may also want to do a deeper assessment and consider challenges/unanswered questions, towering strengths, and the other factors, for now I recommend just focusing on these two primary factors.)

What if you are having difficulty identifying the pivotal positions? It may be that you are having trouble distinguishing critical positions from merely important ones. Perhaps there's disagreement between what the general manager says is pivotal and what other team members perceive as pivotal. The following recommendations will facilitate differentiation:

▲ *Begin by drilling down to the ultimate objective of the change.* Sometimes people focus on surface issues and misidentify who is really going to push the change over the top. For instance, let's say a company wants to merge with another organization. On the surface, the goal is the merger. The ultimate objective, however, has to do with working faster, cheaper, or better in some way. Therefore, the general counsel who set up the nuts and bolts of the merger agreement is important rather than pivotal; it's a technical rather than a pivotal role. A true pivotal position may be the manufacturing vice president who is responsible for achieving the more efficient manufacturing process that is the ultimate objective of the merger.

▲ *Aim for a 10 percent target.* In other words, if there are a hundred different positions in your unit, at least ten of them should be designated as pivotal. Though the number of pivotal positions varies in each situation, my experience tells me that people often overestimate what is pivotal, indicating that 50 percent or more of the positions are crucial. In fact, it's usually around 10 percent. Keeping this fact in mind will help you narrow the field.

▲ *Look at pivotal positions from a negative standpoint.* In other words, imagine a position staffed by someone who not only demonstrated a tremendous resistance to change in the past, but seems as if he would be tremendously rigid if you asked him to take on a larger role or an unfamiliar task. What would be the consequences if you were depending on someone in this position to make change happen? If your answer is, "The consequences would be horrific," then you've found your pivotal position. If you feel the change strategy could still survive weakness at this position, it is probably not pivotal.

As you attempt to make pivotal position decisions, keep in mind that people commit all sorts of errors and fall into various traps as they conduct this assessment piece. Be alert for the following three errors:

1. *Asking many managers for their pivotal position opinions.* If you want to confuse yourself and your team, do a survey of your unit's managers. You'll discover that not only do these managers each have different opinions about what is pivotal, but they tend to list just about every position under the sun. This is the nature of most managers. I know one manager who made a very convincing argument that if a position wasn't pivotal for change, it shouldn't exist. Limit your questions about this issue to the person driving the change, your team, and an HR representative.

2. *Failing to take functional biases into consideration.* If the driver of the change came up through one function and has little exposure to other functions, she may demonstrate a bias in favor of pivotal positions related to her function. The same holds true for you and members of your team. All you can do is be aware of this tendency and make every effort to be functionally objective in your assessment. While HR people can sometimes help achieve this objectivity, they too have their biases and may be pushing for the pivotal positions that management has designated, not necessarily the ones that are relevant to your particular circumstances.

3. *Confusing "who" and "what."* Pivotal positions are a "what," although it's easy to mistake them for a "who." People immediately think of the who—who is indispensable to the change effort? They focus on the person who can make or break the strategy. The problem is that these managers may not occupy pivotal positions. They are singled out, however, because they're highly talented from a technical standpoint or carry a lot of clout. A position focus is a strategic approach. Once you know what positions are going to catalyze change, then you can worry about who will fill them.

Another common mistake comes after pivotal positions are decided upon and present incumbents are listed on the chart. It happens when intelligent and astute managers and

HR people inflate the change response and versatility ratings. They're usually operating in cultures of hope and accommodation, and such cultures encourage wishful thinking and avoid harsh realities. As a result, they're unable to look at these positions with a hard eye. They can't accept the fact that they have a C-player in a pivotal position and use magic thinking to transform him into an A-player. As a result, the pivotal position chart delivers a false message, and your group moves forward believing it has the right people in the right positions. Or, if you are an HR person in the grip of a falsely optimistic culture, you convince members of your team that people will "grow into their pivotal positions." Because you've helped recruit and develop many of the people in the company and watched them grow, you find it difficult to see any of the individuals occupying pivotal positions as less than an A-player.

Functional Depth

As obviously crucial as pivotal positions are, it is a mistake to focus on them exclusively. Any change has ramifications and requirements beyond pivotal areas. It may well be that pivotal positions for a given change are clustered in one or two functions, but that doesn't mean that you can ignore other functions without consequence. Change searches out the weakest point in an organization and starts pressuring that point.

For example, a large multinational corporation attempting to reorganize itself and create a leaner, more flexible structure was hampered not by leadership and strategic positions but by its lack of marketing depth. The corporation did a terrible job selling the restructuring to its stakeholders (including its own people and suppliers), which resulted in a premature breakdown of the restructuring process. The company did not consider any marketing position as pivotal to this change, yet marketing ended up playing a significant support role (or rather, lack-of-support role).

Figure 5-2 is designed to help you assess your organization's functional depth. It is simply a way to reconfigure information you've already gleaned from your personal change

Figure 5-2. Functional Capability Matrix

Future Versatility	Sales	Marketing	Research and Development	Design Engineering	Operations Engineering
Will create growth **Clearly Versatile**					
Will create growth; needs more development **Expandable**					
Solid citizen **Irreplaceable Pro**					
Solid; needs to continue to grow as bar is raised **Well-Placed**					
Limited as to flexibility **Minimally Versatile**					

capacity assessments. By inserting each person assessed into a square on the chart, based on the individual's versatility rating, you can quickly see the functions in which you're strong and the ones where you're weak. Versatility, not change response, is the key factor here. You are assessing for future depth—that is, the capability of people in different functions to take on new and larger roles and responsibilities. While change response is an important factor for depth, versatility is more important. To keep your assessment as simple as possible, therefore, focus only on versatility.

Backups

You can count on at least one of the people you are counting on to leave. You can also assume that backups who might contribute a great deal to a change effort will be stymied. In a volatile environment with a war for talent raging, people come and go with precedent-setting speed, so it's not just your key people that you have to be concerned about.

A simple bit of insurance is to list backup candidates for your pivotal positions and rate their change response and versatility scores (you may have already assessed some of these individuals). You don't need to spend a great deal of time on this activity, but ask your team to do a quick "read" of backup candidates so you can complete this guesstimate ranking.

This is also a worthwhile exercise because you may find that the backup candidates have a higher personal change capacity than the people who occupy pivotal positions. You may determine in the roadmap step (Chapter 6) that your change strategy is better served with a backup candidate in that pivotal position.

Figure 5-3 is a form you can use to make a list of backups for pivotal positions. After you create the list, place one of the following three designations next to each of their names:

▲ *Mismatched.* These backups are A-players ready and eager to expand their roles and take on change projects, but their bosses (those occupying pivotal positions) aren't going

Figure 5-3. Succession Backup Chart

Division/Unit: _____ Date: _____
Function: _____

		Issues
Incumbent Manager/ **Executive:** _____ **Job Title:** _____ **Change Response:** _____ **Versatility:** _____ **Job Date:** _____	**Backups (priority order)** Candidate/Job: (1) _____ (2) _____ (3) _____	_____ _____ _____
Direct Reports:		
Manager/Executive: _____ **Job Title:** _____ **Change Response:** _____ **Versatility:** _____ **Job Date:** _____	**Backups (priority order)** Candidate/Job: (1) _____ (2) _____ (3) _____	_____ _____ _____
Manager/Executive: _____ **Job Title:** _____ **Change Response:** _____ **Versatility:** _____ **Job Date:** _____	**Backups (priority order)** Candidate/Job: (1) _____ (2) _____ (3) _____	_____ _____ _____

anywhere. This can be a problematic situation for a number of reasons, especially if the pivotal people exhibit middle-of-the-road change capacity. It's also a problem if they are denied the opportunity to become more involved in change programs and leave the company.

▲ *Bad timing.* The people in pivotal positions are ready to move up or out, but the backups aren't ready to move in. Their personal change capacities are promising, but they need a certain amount of development and experience before they can make a contribution to the change effort. This is a very common situation in many companies where five people are being groomed as successors for twenty-five positions. This goes back to the point about cultures of hope and accommodation: These companies believe that somehow, someway these five people will provide sufficient backup and that other people who have solid change capacities will be magically unearthed.

▲ *Alignment.* In this situation, a backup is poised to take over when the pivotal person is ready to move on. For instance, Jerry is the head of research and development and he's ready to tackle a nonfunctional staff position. Martha, his backup, is champing at the bit to handle new and expanded responsibilities, and she's responded well to change in the past. This is an ideal situation and, unfortunately, one that's all too rare.

Vulnerability Analysis

Of course, the people you can least afford to lose are your A-players. The question is: How vulnerable are you to losing them?

While you may have touched upon this question earlier when you examined the challenges/unanswered questions related to each individual you are assessing, now is the time to analyze the issue in a more focused manner. By this point, you should have a better idea of who your A-players are now than you did earlier in the process.

Unexpected departures of key people can cripple a change effort faster than anything (especially if you lack adequate backup). One organization in the midst of launching its first new major product line in ten years lost its sales director, marketing vice president, and the line's brand manager within a four-month period. Almost immediately, the new product line introduction faltered. There was a ripple effect as the managers who were being counted on to drive the change disappeared; their replacements didn't have the same high change-response and versatility scores, and they shied away from some of the new initiatives designed to facilitate the introduction. Their resistance was felt by some direct reports whose behaviors and attitudes mirrored those of their bosses.

The point is to anticipate the pivotal people who might leave and take steps to prevent it, or make sure backups are in place if it happens. If you are an HR person or have one on your team, you probably have experience in reading the signs that a star is poised to leave; you've done a hindsight analysis in which you determined why a top performer left and what might have been done to prevent it. This experience will come in handy as the team assesses key people in two important areas:

1. *Marketability.* Every organization has acknowledged stars, and if yours are in key positions (or they are approaching star status), you can bet that executive search firms have contacted them. Marketability, however, is a subjective subject, and you may be overestimating or underestimating an individual's true marketability. To obtain a more objective picture, answer the following questions:

- ▲ Does this person have the type of experience and track record that would impress other organizations?
- ▲ Does he have skills and knowledge that are highly prized in your industry specifically and the marketplace in general?
- ▲ Does she have specific accomplishments that are well known or that clearly establish her high level of performance?

▲ Does the individual demonstrate the type of networking and people skills that yield contacts that in turn lead to job offers?

2. *Satisfaction.* Some key people may be highly marketable yet have no desire to go anywhere else: They're perfectly content to stay right where they are. On the other hand, there are people who are dismally unhappy with what they do and how they do it. You need to separate the satisfied from the dissatisfied as well as determine the underlying sources of dissatisfaction. To this end, answer the following questions:

▲ Does this person seem truly satisfied with his job; if so, why?

▲ If the individual is not satisfied, where does the dissatisfaction stem from (e.g., job responsibilities; relationships with bosses or peers; compensation issues; career progression and opportunities; the way in which the organization, the work group, or the industry is changing)?

If you find that someone with high change-response and versatility scores possesses the double whammy of dissatisfaction and marketability, this may seem like bad news. In fact, it's good news, at least in the sense that forewarned is forearmed. In the roadmap phase of this process, you'll learn what can be done to retain these people.

Significant Personal Change Idiosyncrasies

Significant is the keyword here. Everyone has minor quirks and tendencies when it comes to change.[1] A manager may have great antipathy to any change that has to do with a dress code or anything related to personal expression. Another individual may have moved a great deal as a child and now resists any new position or role that calls on him to increase his travel or spend time in other offices.

All this is par for the course, and you shouldn't become hung up on the psychological nuances of an individual's reaction to change. If you try to analyze all the complex attitudes and behaviors of an individual when it comes to change, you'll become lost in a psychological maze. There are at least twenty useful personal change capacity types, based on combinations of the five versatility and four change response categories discussed in Chapter 3. In reality, however, there are thousands of different attitudes and behaviors in response to and in anticipation of change. They only become usable when filtered through the prism of change response and versatility and when limited to a reasonable number.

That said, it is important to point out that there are some idiosyncratic reactions to change that can seriously undermine otherwise strong personal change capacities. What you need to be alert for are the most common idiosyncrasies. As long as you identify these negative reactions, create a development program to remedy them, or remove this individual from a key role, then you'll have prevented the weakness from doing any harm.

The following is a list of the five most common idiosyncrasies that people display:

1. *Requires strong supervision or structure in the face of change.* Some people are clearly versatile only under tightly structured conditions. In the past, they've demonstrated that they are active responders when they have the security of a boss to advise them or a system that is familiar and comfortable. At the same time, they've also demonstrated that they can be blocked responders without this security. The mistake is to designate people as being clearly versatile and able to take on new roles based only on their active response in certain situations. Be aware that some people handle any type of change poorly if they feel all the familiar support systems and parameters have been removed. You either need to create development programs to resolve this problem or place these people only in roles where they have the security they need.

2. *Responds poorly to a certain type of change.* I know one manager who was a highly effective change agent in every situation except one: He resisted any type of cultural shift. He

had worked for the same company for twenty years and prized the company's culture. When the organization was acquired and new philosophies and political realities began to seep in, he rebelled. Others have problems with changes involving restructuring, resenting the downsizing that sometimes accompanies it or the breakup of a tight-knit team or division. Some people have problems with a certain type of change because they had a bad experience with it in the past; others are philosophically opposed to it. Whatever the reason, you need to be aware of whether the changes you are contemplating will rub one of your key people the wrong way.

3. *Has difficulty handling rapid changes.* Some people are rattled when they are asked to make changes quickly or when change unfolds almost instantly all around them. These same people may deal well with gradual transitions and even take leadership roles in these transitions. But when change happens suddenly—when new ownership comes in and reorganizes immediately or when deadlines for implementing new processes or policies are incredibly tight—they resist. Again, this weakness can be identified when you talk about an individual's change response rating. You simply need to ask your team if someone has had difficulty with change when it takes place quickly.

4. *Shows unwillingness to make "personal" changes.* There are people who seem to be A-players because they've consistently responded positively to a variety of process, political, and policy changes and seem to embrace new roles and responsibilities consistently. The problem is that they are A-players only if change doesn't impact their personal style of working. For instance, Lou was a command-and-control type leader who was incapable of functioning effectively in a team-oriented system. Although he had handled all sorts of changes effectively over the years, he was unable to manage without giving orders. To say Lou was minimally versatile when he was asked to integrate himself into a team environment was putting it mildly. He not only stubbornly clung to his command-and-control mentality, he also bad-mouthed the new system to anyone who would listen. Coaching is a logical de-

velopment recommendation for people who have difficulty making personal changes. The key, however, is spotting this issue in advance, and sometimes even the most perceptive assessors miss it when people have responded so well to nonpersonal changes in the past.

5. *Is overly aggressive in leading change.* While there are some people who fight change tooth and nail, there are others who thrive on new challenges and environments. This is fine in most instances, but there are people who become overly enthusiastic in their change leadership. They try to implement changes too fast; they push their people too hard to make changes in how they work; they use threats and intimidation to push change through the system; they are so enamored of "new and different" that they throw out perfectly good ideas just because they perceive them as stale. Sometimes a little feedback helps this type of change responder calm down and become an effective leader. Sometimes it takes more experience in support roles during change initiatives. Whatever you do, don't underestimate the damage this type of person can cause. If placed in a pivotal position, his single-minded zeal for change can alienate everyone around him.

Identifying the five idiosyncratic reactions to change assumes that your team is very familiar with the individual being evaluated as well as the change being planned. While this is usually a correct assumption, sometimes it's not. In the former case, you may be assessing someone who has just joined the organization or been transferred from another group. Because you lack a manager who has observed and worked with this person over a period of time, you lack the knowledge to make accurate judgments about his change capacity. While one alternative is to interview managers who do know this individual well (either at another company or in another group within your company), this is usually not a good alternative. You are relying on information that may be colored by a manager who resented losing this person or may have catalyzed his exit.

In most instances, however, new people aren't dubbed

key people for a change strategy. If they've just joined the organization, it's doubtful that they're ready to take on a key role. The exception might be if someone has been specifically recruited for this role because she possesses the towering strength that dovetails with the targeted skill required by the change strategy. In this case, the person who recruited her will know enough about her to serve on the team and help with the assessment. If HR personnel were heavily involved in the recruitment process, they may be able to provide some useful insights.

The other issue—the team's familiarity with the changes that will be required—usually isn't a significant issue. Certainly there are changes that are difficult to anticipate. When a merger or acquisition takes place, it is tremendously difficult to project what changes are going to be made. Sometimes you won't be able to predict how a restructuring or other major change process will impact people and what will be required of them. On the other hand, it's not critical you know these things. Part of the value of this assessment is that you are determining personal change capacity, not personal change capacity in a specific situation. You can rely on the change response and versatility ratings alone to give you a fairly accurate read of how people will do in any change situation. Certainly it's worthwhile knowing the specific situation—it increases the degree of accuracy—but in lieu of that knowledge this more general assessment usually suffices.

Much Ado about Something

Analyzing weak links isn't as time-consuming or as difficult as you might imagine. Brief team discussions or conversations with bosses often reveal these weak links, especially when you know what to look for. When you understand that you need to examine pivotal positions, functional depth, vulnerability to losing key people, and idiosyncratic change reactions, you have already clearly defined areas to consider.

Organizations that have dealt effectively with change—companies such as General Electric, ADT Security Services,

Baxter International, Johnson & Johnson, Bank of America, Citibank, and Federal Express—are vigilant against these weak links. They recognize that change is carried forward on the backs of individuals, and that the more they know about each individual's weaknesses (as well as strengths), the better they can help remedy these flaws and place people in the roles that will benefit the change process.

What's shocking is that most managers move their groups into the change maelstrom armed only with performance reviews and that HR goes along with this action. The information they possess about an individual's weak areas is supposedly contained in these reviews. In fact, performance reviews are generally worthless in this regard (and in other regards as well). The upshot of most performance reviews is that the employee is slightly above average. You may get a sense of the individual's skills and where her performance has come up short, but there's nothing in a performance review that explains the employee's shortcomings relative to change issues. What's also missing is all the "context" data that's been covered in this chapter. It is positively criminal that a manager going into a change effort doesn't have the vaguest notion whether key people might leave tomorrow or if they will respond to change in a way that may be destructive.

Managing people in a status quo environment is like playing checkers. Managing them in the face of change is like playing chess. Too many managers remain in the checkers mode. They ask simple questions: How can I motivate Joan to help me get everyone excited about the new process? There's nothing wrong with this question, but it ignores all the other questions. Is Joan in a pivotal position? Is she a good backup for the person who is in the pivotal position? Is Joan likely to leave the organization soon and, if she does leave, who do we have to take her place effectively? Does she have an idiosyncratic reaction to change that might prove harmful?

With all this information in hand, you can use it to create an effective, change-focused plan for your people.

6

Drawing the Roadmap

Individual assessment concludes by mapping out a direction for key people. By now, you have assessed their personal change capacity and should have a good sense of their change response and versatility ratings, as well as the five factors—targeted skills, pivotal positions, towering strengths, development needs, and challenges/unanswered questions—that impact this change capacity. You have assembled profiles that you've translated into a group change capacity assessment. At the same time, you've gathered additional information about possible weak links, such as pivotal positions and backup strength, that might weaken your change strategy if left unaddressed.

Now you are ready to set a course based on this information. To implement whatever change most concerns your group, you need to decide who should lead the change effort, who should follow, and who should get out of the way (or be gently pushed to the side). You need to determine whether you really have enough talent on board to handle the responsibilities and tasks that this particular change demands. You need to assess which individuals to develop to maximize their change capacity, or you may need to hire or "borrow" the talent necessary to make change happen.

The roadmap you'll create in this chapter is outlined in Figure 6-1. The roadmap process will give you guidance in setting a direction and moving on to the individual development square of the change matrix discussed at the beginning of this book in the Introduction (see Figure I-1). The first part of this mapping exercise involves making a go or no-go deci-

Figure 6-1. The Roadmap

> **5. Develop a Go-Forward Plan**
> ▲ Detail the Change Scenario
> ▲ Document People Issues and Implications
> ▲ Ensure Organization Preparedness
> ▲ Create Individual Plans for Key Talent

> **4. Road Warnings**
> ▲ Ensure Objectivity with Judgments

> **3. Moving Forward with Routes Mapped**

> **2. Individual Action Planning and Identifying**
> ▲ Who Needs Development
> ▲ Key Challenges/Unanswered Questions
> ▲ Career Management Issues

> **1. Stoplight Analysis**
> ▲ Analyze the Total Picture
> ▲ Test Future Business Scenarios

sion based on the people you have and the change you're attempting to implement.

Stoplight Analysis

You need to put the names of the people you've assessed on green, yellow, and red index cards and either post them on a board or lay them out on a table for your team to see and discuss. Each card corresponds to the colors of a stoplight, green being a signal that someone is ready to move on and assume change-based responsibilities, yellow a caution about that person relative to change, and red a clear sign that you should stop this person before it's too late. This visual device may seem unnecessary—in fact, you may feel that your previous analysis of each person's change capacity is far more sophisticated—but you'll find that grouping people in this way facilitates your team's decision making.

What you are actually doing is taking your A-, B-, C-, and D-players and moving them from four individual assessment categories into three "group" categories. While most of your A-players and B-players will be grouped in the green category, and C-players will be yellow and D-players red, it's useful to reshuffle the deck using these cards. This exercise will not only provide you with a fail-safe mechanism to double-check your initial assessments, but it offers you a fresh perspective on whether you have the people to go forward with the change, or whether you must proceed with caution or stop and reassess altogether. The use of color cards is an immediate and simple way to do a reality check. When you categorize someone as red, yellow, or green, you want to make sure that the label is the right one.

Here's how to assign an individual the right color:

▲ *Green.* To start, refer back to Chapter 4, Figure 4-2, and look at the names you wrote in the four boxes in the upper right-hand corner of the group change capacity matrix. This corner of the matrix identifies active and passive responders and clearly versatile and expandable people. These people are the best candidates to shine during a change effort—they are your A-players and B-players. While active responders and clearly versatile individuals are usually a lock for receiving a green rating, you may have some doubts about people who are passive responders and expandable. When in doubt, pay attention to the challenges/unanswered questions you've noted for a given individual as well as the weak links. For example, you may find that Linda has a history of responding with too much aggression when given supervisory roles for change efforts. Or you may see that Terry deals well with change when he's in a structured environment with a strong supervisor, but he has problems in unstructured situations. Or you may question whether Jim can develop the towering strengths required by your strategic time frame. These questions and weak links can tip the balance between a green and yellow designation. It is also important to remember that people given a green designation aren't always immediately ready to become change agents. Some of them may need a bit of development or additional experience before they are ready. In other words, it's fine to place potential change stars in this category.

▲ *Yellow.* These people cluster toward the center of the matrix. They're well-placed or irreplaceable pros with limited versatility. Their change response rating is often reactive (and sometimes passive). These are the solid citizens you can count on for support during periods of change, but you can't count on them for leadership or for taking on significantly increased roles and responsibilities. In many instances, these individuals will possess critical towering strengths—strengths that will serve your group well as the change process unfolds—but their role will be self-limited. Give people a yellow flag if they have demonstrated dependability in the face of change but an inability to step outside their area of expertise or to embrace a challenge they've never encountered before. The yellow warning flag signifies that you shouldn't expect too much from these people as change unfolds; if you expect too much, you are going to find that they hurt rather than help achieve your change goals.

▲ *Red.* These individuals are minimally versatile and reactive or blocked change responders—you'll find their names listed in the lower left-hand corner of the matrix. It's relatively easy to red-card individuals who are obviously misplaced and blocked; they stand out like sore thumbs when you see how resistant they are to change. The problem is determining if the reactive, minimally versatile individual belongs here or in the yellow-card group. You'll find that some of these people have significant towering strengths. They are technically skilled often, and you are eager to use these skills as you transform your piece of the organization. But these people may be so averse to any change in their environment, or so resistant to trying a new approach, that their skills will be rendered useless by their negative attitudes. Individuals who've been given a red flag pose a real threat to whatever new program or initiative you are pursuing. Put individuals in this group when you are convinced they will contribute nothing or you suspect that their contributions will be minimal.

Once you post these cards for your team to peruse, do a reality check. In other words, take a step back and ask, "Can we really count on John (designated green) to leave his office and take a proactive role in motivating his direct reports to maximize the new system?" Open up a question for discussion and debate. If you followed the steps for assigning the color codes, you'll find that most people have been accurately color-coded and that your initial judgment is accurate. Still, it's wise to do this final check before you commit to a decision to depend on someone to lead change—or before you exclude someone from having any significant role in your group.

To double-check your color-coding process, do the following:

▲ *Review an individual's recent behaviors and actions, especially those that might have occurred since you first started the change capacity assessment.* It may be that someone has recently done or said something that contradicts the color tag you've given him. For instance, you assigned Steve a yellow card, yet he recently showed great initiative in proposing a plan to revamp all the jobs in the department. If your team agrees that there is a significant gap between your ratings and how the individual has behaved recently, then you should reconsider your rating.

▲ *Go back to your original change response and versatility ratings and determine if someone was on the cusp.* Were you struggling to determine if Joe was clearly versatile or expandable? If you rated Jill a passive responder, was it a unanimous decision or was there some debate among team members about this change response issue? It may be that you erred in one direction or the other because someone was on the borderline. In that case, now is the time to make a correction.

▲ *Rely on the judgment of team members who have done change capacity assessments before.* Some companies routinely place certain human resources (HR) people on assessment teams, and they become in-house change capacity experts. You may be that expert or else you've selected someone from HR to work on your team. The other team members can turn to this individual if they are in doubt about what color code is appropriate for a given individual.

What Are the Larger Implications?

On the most basic level, you can immediately make some judgments about future direction based on how many people you have in each color category. At one extreme, if you have mostly green cards, you know you are overloaded with talent for whatever change you need to implement (or if you have mostly red cards, you know you're in bad shape). If you have a good mix of green and yellow cards—the ideal scenario—then you are well-stocked in change leaders and supporters who will serve your group's needs well.

By a quick look at the color distribution, you can answer the critical question: "What are the implications for our change strategy?" It may signal that "we're in trouble," or it can suggest that the organization needs to develop certain people to make the change effort work, or it might send the message that recruiting is necessary to obtain talent. It's a sobering experience to see how the colors lie out on a board. At ADT, in the early days, the senior management team looked at the cards and said, "I hate to say this, but with the people we have, there's no way we can make this [acquisition] work." You may also discover that you are better off than you thought. Another company found that although the majority of cards were yellow, it still had a few solid green ones. Initially, the company assumed that it would have to borrow (outsource) or buy (recruit) the talent it needed to expand its presence in a market. In reality, it only had to use a few outside companies and was able to develop its own green-rated people into effective change leaders.

These card-based evaluations are useful whether you are trying to make incremental changes in your unit or are thinking in organizationwide terms. Speaking of large-scale change, Federal Express was at one point considering expanding into the passenger business. From a strategic and technological standpoint, this expansion made sense. Federal Express already had the cargo planes and had found a way to convert them economically into passenger planes. Many of the top people at Federal Express were excited about this move.

But the move never took place. While there were a number of factors that influenced this decision, the most significant one had to do with talent. When Federal Express did an assessment similar to the one I'm suggesting here (I was working at Federal Express at the time), we discovered that we lacked enough A-players to make this change work. We had people who were highly skilled in the overnight-package transportation business, but many of them didn't have the personal change capacity necessary to take on new and expanded roles or deal with all the changes the passenger market would demand. While we were well-stocked with irreplaceable pros (yellow cards) and possessed some people who were active responders and clearly versatile, we still were coming up short. Our options—to recruit, develop, or use outside sources—weren't feasible for many reasons, the main one being the lack of time. If we were going to expand, we had to expand soon or the window of opportunity would close. Thus, this initially exciting expansion strategy never saw the light of day.

Testing Change-Based Scenarios

Testing future business scenarios is a highly effective technique to determine whether your talent measures up to the changes that are required. What you want to do is test at least two linked scenarios in the following way:

1. *Write a brief description that captures the change-based scenario that you foresee in the future.* It may be making a preemptive move in the marketplace, merging with another group, or introducing a new product or service. Describe this scenario and the changes people will have to make to deal

with it—for example, describe with as much specificity as possible the new roles and responsibilities and the leadership that
must be displayed.

2. *Determine whether this change effort is an internal or
external scenario, and then link it to its counterpart.* In other
words, an external change scenario might be establishing a
sales presence in a new market. The linked internal scenario
might involve creating a new customer service center to accommodate the demands of this new market. You want to explore these two linked scenarios because one scenario is often
insufficient. You may go into a change confident that you have
the talent to establish a strong sales presence in a new market,
but you may find that your talent for managing a new customer
service center is nonexistent. Because most change has both
internal and external impact, you want to evaluate your talent
in terms of both scenarios.

3. *Run these scenarios past a gauntlet of talent questions.*
The type of talent you need depends on the type of change you
need to make. Some groups don't need to make huge changes;
they don't need many or even any green-card types because
their changes are mostly technical in nature, and therefore a
solid core of yellow-card irreplaceable pros and well-placed
individuals will suffice. In other instances, you may need a
strong base of change leaders who are designated green and
are ready to go. You also want to filter in the other issues
you've assessed for—towering strengths, pivotal positions,
backup strength, and other weak links—into the mix. The goal
is to make all this information actionable on an individual
basis. To that end, have your team subject the two scenarios to
the following questions:

    ▲ In each of these scenarios, what type of changes do we
      need to make, and does our talent base seem capable
      of making them?
    ▲ If we are falling short, is it in our external or internal
      scenario (or both)?
    ▲ Do we possess the towering strengths that are crucial
      for the changes required by these scenarios?

▲ Are the people in pivotal positions what we need, given the demands of each scenario?

▲ Do we possess the bench strength necessary to implement and manage the requisite changes should our frontline people leave?

▲ Are we particularly vulnerable to losing any of the key people we are depending on to make change happen?

▲ Have we considered any *major* personal change idiosyncrasies that might have a significant impact on our evaluation? (The word *major* is emphasized because everyone has change idiosyncrasies, and your team should only concern itself with ones that seem to pose serious obstacles, given the change strategy involved.)

Once you've answered these questions, you'll have a very good sense if you possess the talent necessary to drive at least two types of change. As you might guess, most people discover that they are not in perfect shape; they don't have the luxury of just sitting back, doing nothing, and watching the change unfold problem free. But whatever the problems might be, you are now at a distinct advantage when it comes to solving them. You've done a holistic assessment, so you are acutely aware of the talent you possess and the talent you lack in relation to the change your group needs to make. Given this assessment, the next step is plotting direction for each person identified through your stoplight analysis.

Individual Action Planning

Much of the individual assessment and development that takes place in organizations is done in a vacuum. Not only aren't people assessed for their change capacity, but they're not developed in ways designed to achieve a group's change goals. Instead, arbitrary judgments are made: Mark is weak in leadership skills, or Sue needs to take an executive development course to better manage the change and chaos all around her. None of these judgments are tied into the big picture. Do we really need Mark to be a leader of change? Is his change capacity such that he should be a leader? Does the change strategy we need to implement give Sue time to develop, or do we have to bring someone else in who can hit the ground running?

Those of you who are HR professionals at large or even midsize organizations are well aware of why this happens: The issues you face are huge and the systems in place aren't designed to link development and change capacity on an individual level. I know several HR directors who were appalled when it was suggested that they develop people with an eye toward change capacity needs. At this time, most assessments are geared toward a skills profile. What is missing in leading change is a way to assess against the key question, "Can this individual drive change?" That is the question asked in corporations, not, "How skilled are they in general?" On the surface, it sounds like an assessment and development nightmare. And it would be without a process to follow. This process not only makes change capacity assessment and development doable, it makes it manageable.

At this point, managing the process means deciding what actions are necessary for each person who has been assessed. For instance, a major corporation was embarking on an ambitious revamping of its distribution system, and a key strategic element in this revamping was designing a software program that would send the right information to the right people at the right time. Designing this new software was as much a strategic problem as a design one; it would require serious thought about who should get what type of information and about providing suppliers with sensitive data. The head of information technology (IT) at this company was obviously in a pivotal position for the change, but he was solidly yellow. As brilliant as he was at designing systems, he was not particularly comfortable with strategy. In the past, he'd resisted strategic shifts, going so far as to tell his top direct reports in one situation that "if we ignore this tangent, perhaps it will go away." His versatility was projected as middle-of-the-road. As an irreplaceable pro, he'd always been good at taking on new responsibilities within his functional area, but he'd also demonstrated an aversion to applying his expertise into areas such as marketing and operations. The assessment team concluded that he would have difficulty taking on a true leadership role, one where he'd be asked to think and plan cross-functionally.

When the team met and talked about the action planning for this IT head in light of two change scenarios, they had a "get real" discussion. One member of the team at first suggested that the IT manager would rise to the challenge—that he would realize more was being asked of him and he would use his considerable skill to tackle the strategic issues. But after some discussion—and after looking at why the team had rated him as it did in terms of change response and versatility—it was clear that his value was limited when it came to the change scenario. In fact, the team agreed that he would probably overrate his ability to deal with the strategic ramifications and give his boss a false sense of confidence if asked if he could handle it. The team members decided that the best course of action was to bring in someone as the new head of IT (and do it quickly) who was strategically adept. Because they didn't want to lose this irreplaceable pro's expertise, they would find a spot for him that was suited to his skills and continue to give him opportunities to grow within the company. A retention plan was necessary to keep him from bolting, and a team member was assigned that responsibility.

To do individual action planning for the people you've assessed through the stoplight (i.e., color card) analysis, you need to:

1. *Determine who needs development, the priority of that development plan, and what the focus of a plan should be.* Remember, you are not creating the development plan at this point, but quickly and concisely setting a development direction. For instance, David may be a green card, which signifies he is someone pivotal to your change effort, but you know he needs some coaching before he's ready to assume an expanded role—he's potentially going to be responsible for an office in Hong Kong and will be making numerous trips there. Obviously, this is a high-priority plan; you need David up to speed within the next year. The focus of the plan is to help David

learn to be confident in his ability to manage a more diverse group of people than he has previously managed.

2. *Examine whether there are challenges/unanswered questions facing your people.* As your group or organization changes, your people will be affected in a variety of ways. You need to anticipate and prepare for the issues they'll face, especially if they are going to play an important or expanded role as the changes occur. Here are some common challenges/questions and the actions that need to be taken in response to them:

▲ Lana, a well-placed manager in the yellow group, is a veteran employee who is going to become nervous and upset as things change. She has been with the organization for years and always bridles when new or different initiatives are introduced. Still, she's extremely competent, and the organization wants to keep her in place. Her boss needs to provide her with feedback and reassurance, explaining why the company is changing and how she will continue to be a valued part of the organization.

▲ Marcia is a young, fast-track executive in the green group. She's launched a number of marketing innovations in the short time she's been with the company, and her towering strengths combined with her strong personal change capacity mark her as a future leader in the months ahead. It's likely that Marcia has been contacted by headhunters about other jobs; the organization is vulnerable to losing her. The company's action response must be to send her a strong retention message. A top executive must reassure her as well as provide her with a sense of how she can quickly move up in the organization; a financial incentive package would also be appropriate.

▲ Mitch is in the red group, assessed as having limited versatility/well-placed and being a blocked change responder. The big question surrounding Mitch is whether he's going to cause trouble when he learns that he is being moved aside as his group is restructured. Given his past response to changes of this type, it's likely that he'll be resentful or angry. Mitch's boss needs to provide him with some straight feedback and work out some options for Mitch to consider. Because he does have some skills that are worth keeping, transferring Mitch to a more appropriate assignment should be one option. Another is letting him go. Above all else, the organization doesn't want Mitch to respond with morale-damaging anger and alienate other people with whom he works, especially during the transition period.

3. *Address career management issues.* There may be some overlap with previous aspects of your assessment, but it's important to make sure you cover these issues. Career-related problems can easily slip through the cracks during chaotic periods of change, and they may weaken the contribution of a green- or yellow-card individual. Be especially attentive for the following career issues relative to the people you've assessed:

▲ *Retirement readiness.* Many times, valuable veteran employees look at the change occurring all around them and say, "I've had enough." You don't want to get caught short when someone you are depending on decides "suddenly" to leave. If you suspect that a green- or yellow-card individual might retire soon, you need to have a talk with her immediately and ascertain her intentions.

▲ *Need for job challenge.* Some of the people you've rated in the yellow or even red category might have received higher ratings a few years ago. For any number of reasons, however, their response to change has become more lackluster and their versatility has diminished. It may be that they are just burned out on a particular job. They've been doing it so long, they've just lost interest. What they need is a new assignment to revitalize them. If you believe that someone is suffering from job burnout and that a significant role in the change effort might produce good results, you may want to take a chance on providing such a challenge.

▲ *Problems with the boss.* Some people may be highly rated, but you're concerned about their future performance because of friction with their boss. If they continue to report to the same person, their contributions to change programs will be limited. Perhaps the boss will prevent them from taking on new assignments and an expanded role, or the tension will grow so great that they'll either leave the company or become so angry or anxious that they won't be able to deliver under the pressure of change. In these instances, your action might be to move them away from this boss and to an environment where they can perform more effectively.

Moving Forward with All Your Routes Mapped

As you create action plans, expect a range of issues and needs to emerge. Ideally, you'll discover that some people are ready right now to assume the new roles that change demands or to provide the support your group is going to require. In other instances, you may find that a red-card person has no place in your group as it evolves, and you need to decide whether you can move him to another group or must let him go. Sometimes, you won't know what to do with a given individual. In these instances, it's useful to create a category called "holding pattern." Typically, these are yellow cards—that is, your solid performers who aren't ready or able to lead the change effort and whose technical skills aren't crucial to the group's plans. Still, they are talented and you don't want to lose them because you might be able to use their talents—you just don't know how. For the moment, it's fine to put them in limbo and wait to see what develops (when you see what happens with your group or organization, you will have a better idea about the role these people should play and their related development needs).

The stoplight analysis will also provide you with some additional directions beyond these individual actions. As you start figuring out what needs to be done with each person assessed, you'll find that these decisions trigger other actions.

The central question that's usually (or should be) asked in team meetings is, "What does this mean to us?" For instance: What does it mean if we have a solid core of irreplaceable pros and well-placed people but we don't have a "green" individual—that is, someone at the ready—for the most pivotal position in our change effort? What it means is that you had better recruit someone fast.

Here are some other meanings that often emerge at this stage in the process:

▲ *Time is short, and so is our supply of talented people.* Time frame issues often pop out after you've examined the cards. When you begin talking about how many people you need to develop and how many you have to recruit, it becomes clear that you can't do everything by the time you need to do it. If, for instance, you only have two months to implement your part of the company's strategy, it becomes clear that given your lack of green- and yellow-card designations, there's no way you can solve this problem through development alone.

▲ *We need to conduct a search.* When you lack people for pivotal positions and development doesn't seem to be the answer, you need to recruit. This may be an immediate need or it may be only a potential one. I've been involved with a number of companies that routinely conduct "opportunistic" searches. They anticipate that they might need some people down the road for changes they are contemplating. For instance, your company is considering moving into a new market and wants a search firm to keep its eye out for a certain type of manager in that market. This way, you are better prepared when a trend emerges or a management decision is made to staff up with people who could handle the new assignment.

▲ *We need to prepare HR to move in the direction of the change strategy.* If you are the HR business partner on your team, you need to take an assertive stance when you meet with your boss. Specifically, you should talk in very concrete terms about how and why HR has to become more change responsive in its practices. In many organizations, HR is always playing catch-up with the business needs of the company. It's scrambling to beef up training in an area that's becoming increasingly important to the company or to hire a specific type of expertise that is essential if the company wants to be a player in a new industry. If you don't have much sway with the HR group, you may feel as if you can't make much of an impact here. It is likely, however, that your lobbying efforts, combined with those of other HR leaders on other change capacity assessment teams, might help HR shift its practices. Sometimes it is even necessary to do an end run to a senior executive to catalyze action. While this can be politically dangerous, it can also be a gamble worth taking. One midsize, low-tech company was poised to target a more sophisticated customer base and, in one of its business change scenarios, realized that the talent it had on board was insufficient to deal with growing IT needs. The few people on staff who were experts in this area were mostly blocked change responders who had well-placed versatility scores; they weren't going to lead the charge in this new area. A few HR people met with the company's COO and communicated what they had concluded. HR focus was dated—most of the resources were directed toward transactional activities that could easily be outsourced. Sadly enough, the HR head was missing an opportunity to align and support the key business strategy. The company's CEO then met with the HR director and told him that HR needed to start developing expertise in recruiting IT people and establishing a solid rewards and recognition system to keep them. The CEO commended the director's HR people who had identified this situation.

Road Warnings

Creating this roadmap is not without its hazards. One obvious danger is that your team is not objective in its assessments and thus in its decision making. This is a significant problem in organizations with "cultures of accommodation" (i.e., where assessments are artificially inflated) and where political game playing is rampant (i.e., where assessments are biased).

   One executive group was assessing employees in anticipation of a major restructuring, and the head of this group was egalitarian to a fault; he tended to defer to whoever felt the strongest about an issue. As a result, the roadmap decisions of this group didn't jibe with the personal change capacity assessments. Instead, people were being developed, reassigned, and placed in pivotal positions according to the vested interests of biased team members. When the restructuring took place, certain groups were filled with green-card-rated people while others were dominated by red cards. This inequitable distribution of talent made it difficult for any of the new groups to cope with change—the red group resisted it and the green group was overloaded with people who wanted to lead it.

Unless you're the CEO, the head of HR, or another top executive, there's only so much you can do to defuse the impact of these issues. Still, here are the measures I've found help ensure a fair assessment and decision-making process:

▲ Choose team members who you know to be honest and objective over those who may have more clout or seniority.

▲ Communicate to the team that if you believe people are making assessment decisions based on favoritism or any other agendas, you will immediately remove them from the team.

▲ Lead team meetings in a way that no one team member is pressured to go along with the majority opinion; work toward decisions by consensus rather than by intimidation.

The second hazard of the roadmap is that people become "branded." In other words, they are forever stamped as a red card and it negatively affects their career in the company. Or, more significantly, a yellow-card individual who has great technical skills resents his card color and leaves the company for one that he feels is more appreciative of his talent.

While the results of this assessment should be confidential—and you should make that clear to team members—word of who received what color rating (or their A-, B-, C-, or D-player rating) can leak out. If this happens, you can often repair some of the damage in the feedback session that's part of the next phase of this process. During feedback, you can communicate to offended parties (at least those you want to retain) that you value their contributions and that you are designing a development plan to help them move up in these change-focused ratings.

Perhaps the biggest danger, however, is creating the roadmap in a naively optimistic way. Like an explorer who hopes and prays his ship is seaworthy enough to make it through dangerous, uncharted waters, some managers trust that their people will sail easily through change programs. Typically, this attitude manifests itself during team discussions of people based on their color-card rating. One manager will say, "Rick may seem like a red card—he may have been a blocked responder in the past—but I've thought about it and Rick strikes me as a solid guy we can count on. I'm sure he'll respond to the challenge when his group begins the new project."

It won't happen, at least not if you naively assume that someone with low personal change capacity will suddenly become highly change responsive and versatile. Again, cultures of hope and accommodation foster this type of thinking, and it results in people being asked to expand their roles and handle new responsibilities—roles and responsibilities that simply are beyond their current capacity. It's possible that they might provide some value to the change effort if their roles are limited. And it's possible that they might be developed in ways that enhance their personal change capacities. But hope alone won't cut it during times of change.

Here's a simple suggestion to avoid these and other roadblocks: Make sure you document the roadmap directions. Don't just keep them in your head. In the next phase of this process, you're going to make critical development decisions about your people and provide them with feedback. To help increase their personal change capacity over the long haul and maximize their current capacity during upcoming periods of organizational change, you need to have easy access to your roadmap directions.

Develop a Go-Forward Plan

Use the following list to summarize your team's roadmap discussions and document your assessment conclusions:

1. Detail the change scenario affecting your group or company (ideally, your team will be able to do this both from a managerial as well as an HR perspective) by noting:

▲ The targeted skills and pivotal positions required by this scenario
▲ The time frames

2. Given this change scenario and your stoplight analysis, list the overall people issues and implications; for example:

▲ Determine if you have the talent necessary to achieve your change goals.
▲ If you do have the talent (or if you are close to what you need), identify the issues that concern you (e.g., weak links, challenges/unanswered questions, towering strengths, and development needs) and how you will address them.
▲ If you don't have the talent, determine whether it makes sense to buy or recruit what you need, given your time frame and financial resources.

3. Specify the nonindividual actions you need to take (or that you will recommend the organization should take) to make change happen, such as:

▲ Recruiting (using search firms)
▲ Outsourcing
▲ Implementing HR system improvements

4. Create a brief go-forward plan for the individuals you've assessed, addressing the following areas:

▲ Feedback based on personal change capacity assessment (the assumption being that feedback will help the individual become aware of a change capacity deficit and work to correct it)

▲ Development

▲ Coaching

▲ A move to a new position (either one with more or new responsibilities for change or potentially one with less responsibilities)

▲ A move out of the company (termination)

▲ Weak links (steps to build depth, respond to idiosyncratic change types, correctly identify pivotal positions, or retain key people you're vulnerable to losing)

All of these recommendations are relatively straightforward. Nonetheless, let's provide an example of how to document roadmap item number 4—the go-forward plan—from the previous list. This sample roadmap explains some of the actions planned for a given individual. As you'll see, these roadmap directions are necessarily brief; you'll fill in the detail during the development phase discussed in Part Two of this book.

Sample Go-Foward Plan for John Jones

▲ *Feedback.* John's boss must make John aware of his need for development and also needs to discuss his change capacity rating. John is a limited versatility/well-placed and reactive responder. Given this rating, John can't take on a larger role or more responsibility as part of a change effort. In the next stage of this process, a detailed plan has to be worked out to increase John's change capacity.

▲ *Development.* There's a high-priority need for a program that will develop John's communication skills and cultural awareness—targeted skills required for the change initiative.

▲ *Coaching.* None is needed at this time.

▲ *Move to new position.* Not required.

▲ *Move out of the company.* Not required.

▲ *Weak links.* In the development program in the next stage, address John's change idiosyncrasy. He has trouble with personal change (e.g., communicating more clearly and more often, learning to work with people from different cultures).

You are now well prepared to develop people in order to maximize their change capacity and energize them about taking on key roles that support and drive change. You're moving into the development stage with a certain amount of knowledge—not only about what a specific individual should do, but what all your key people must do to achieve group and organizational change objectives.

Part Two

Creating a Development and Coaching Plan

7

Setting the Stage for Successful, Change-Focused Development

Now that you know what people need to do to become successful change agents, how do you get them to do it? While you've created an individual development plan that clearly communicates what each person needs to do to become a valuable member of the change team, there is no guarantee that they'll do it.

This second phase of the process is designed to increase the odds that your people will follow the development plan you've established for them. While it's likely that at least one person in your group will enthusiastically follow his plan and increase his change capacity as a result, it's also likely that others will resist or not pursue it as vigorously as they might. Veteran human resources people know that plunging directly into development is not always a good idea. If you are in human resources (HR), you can tell stories about well-conceived development plans that never developed anything but dust. To reduce the odds of failure, follow these four steps that end in successful, change-focused development:

1. Create an environment conducive to development.
2. Offer feedback based on the results of the personal change capacity assessment.

3. Choose the development options that meet individual needs.
4. Provide coaching that facilitates personal change capacity development.

The focus of this chapter is on step 1—creating a conducive environment. Let's begin by understanding what you can do to influence the environment in which you're asking people to work on change-based skills, behaviors, and attitudes.

Take an Overall Environmental Reading and Adjust the Climate in Your Area

If you are working in a culture of accommodation, recognize that this culture saps individual initiative.[1] While you probably lack the power to change the overall culture, you can do a number of things to create a new, healthier culture within your group or, as an HR professional, impact everything from training to rewards and recognition systems.

Begin by determining what type of culture you have. Take some time to reflect on the values and beliefs of your organization. Many managers—especially managers who have been with an organization for a significant period of time—take their company's policies for granted, failing to recognize how the status quo is affecting people's response to change.

To help you determine if you are working in a culture of accommodation, here are the ten signs of such a culture. If you recognize less than four of these signs, your culture is probably conducive to change. If you recognize more than seven, you are going to find that people will not be particularly invested in or energized by the development plan you've created. If there are four to seven signs, there's a fifty-fifty chance that individuals will resist development. See how many of the following ten signs apply to your company:

1. A disproportionate amount of time is spent by employees complaining about what the company has done/not done for them.

2. Promotion is primarily based on tenure.
3. An ideology of "who is here" as opposed to "what do we need" is pervasive.
4. If work is not done, it goes to the next highest level; mediocrity is accepted or glossed over.
5. Real feedback is rare and people are treated with kid gloves.
6. Past practices drive employee behavior much more than present best practices and future needs.
7. Issues are not addressed—a "conspiracy of politeness" dominates how people behave, though nasty infighting and political game playing go on behind closed doors.
8. There is little turnover, though everyone knows that certain individuals are poor performers.
9. Technical specialists are commonly promoted into management positions and often block the energies and talents of those working under them.
10. People feel frustrated about their jobs.

Even in this type of culture, however, development is possible. If you find that your company exhibits some or all of these signs, you can still influence your group's environment in ways that fight against this culture and foster development by doing the following:

▲ *Act immediately upon the results of your group's personal change capacity assessment.* Don't delay implementation of development plans based on the assessment because you don't take the results seriously or believe that the solution to your change challenge lies in "financials" or technology. You want to communicate to your direct reports (who participated in the assessment) that people's change capacity is a critical issue. If you are an HR member of the assessment team, encourage line managers to act quickly. Volunteer your training resources and expertise to help implement the plans.

▲ *Promote people into pivotal positions based on change capacity rather than technical expertise.* Likewise, move people out of these positions if their change capacity is low.

▲ *Level with people about both their change capacity strengths and weaknesses.* People are usually more resilient than you might give them credit for.

▲ *Share information about the change strategy.* Explain to people not only what it means to the company, but its relevance to your group and each individual member.

You can take these actions in many different ways to create a beneficial environment. But perhaps the best and more important thing you can do is communicate that you mean business. While you may not have formally announced that you are conducting a personal change capacity assessment, word of it has probably leaked. Your key people need to understand that change capacity is a critical variable not only for their individual future success but the success of the group. Too often, people are cynical. They believe that no matter what their bosses say, it's still going to be business as usual. You need to take a specific action to jar them into recognizing the new reality.

Create Instability and Energy

To help your people increase their change capacity and develop skills, behaviors, and attitudes geared for a specific change strategy, you need to demonstrate that both you and your organization are serious. While you can and should communicate the seriousness of the situation in words, you also need to demonstrate it by your actions. Most people won't make the commitment to development that you require unless they are convinced that there's a compelling reason to make that commitment. In the larger sense, you and other managers need to "unfreeze" the organization and convince everyone that new positional movement is taking place. In your area, you have to create energy and a sense that the old rules no longer apply (i.e., a level of instability). Or if you occupy an HR position, you need to support the efforts of your team members by seeking resources and system changes from HR to shake things up.

Specifically, here are four critical actions managers should take and HR people should support relative to A-, B-, C-, and D-players. Some of these actions may occur simultaneously with the feedback and development steps of the process:

1. *Move the D-players.* This can mean anything from outplacement to transferring them to another group to taking away certain roles and responsibilities. At one organization, Steve was a veteran marketing manager who had been assessed as a D-player. Over the years, he had become increasingly complacent and unwilling to take new chances with brand positioning and had stuck with the same advertising and sales promotion agencies for years, even though their performance was lackluster. Early in his career with the company, Steve had helped introduce a new product that had done tremendously well, and his success with this product (which continued to sell over the years) seemed to cement his hold on his job. Steve's boss, however, realized that Steve had become a luxury. The company had just acquired a European firm and one ramification of the acquisition was a new line of products to be introduced domestically. The company required dramatic, risk-taking marketing for these products to break through. When Steve was let go, everyone in the marketing department became more responsive to the feedback and development plans presented to them.

Please understand that I'm not advocating "making an example" of someone just to create instability and energy. But if you do have a D-player working for you, you need to move him sideways, down, or out.

2. *Challenge C-players with improvement goals.* Many times, C-players are technically proficient, and everyone has assumed that their technical proficiency would safeguard their jobs. C-players need to be put on notice that their technical proficiency is insufficient to guarantee them anything in a changing workplace. They need to understand that they have to develop a new skill, change a negative attitude, or improve their overall change capacity if they expect to have a future in your group.

This message doesn't have to be communicated negatively. Make it clear that there's a reward waiting for them if
they meet the goals you set for them. But if they don't, you
need to take action quickly. If their technical expertise is truly
valuable, carve out a role for them where they aren't asked
to take on new and unfamiliar tasks that they're incapable of
handling. It may be that you have to remove them from pivotal
positions and confine their roles to something that is purely
technical in nature. If you can do without their expertise,
move them in the same way you did D-players.

3. *Re-recruit B-players.* While you may feel you are creating a lot of negative energy with your actions toward C-players
and D-players, you can generate a great deal of positive energy
depending on how you handle A-players and B-players. It is
likely that B-players have felt undervalued and underutilized;
they may have believed that their willingness to take risks, to
be innovative, and to take on new assignments hasn't been
appreciated. While they probably aren't quite ready to assume
pivotal positions in the change effort, they may play crucial
support roles and assume leadership positions in time.

Demonstrate this fact to them and enlist them in helping
your group make change happen. Hold out the carrot of pivotal
positions if they develop in specific ways or if they help answer unanswered questions. Even better, increase their responsibilities and broaden their roles to take advantage of
their above-average change capacity. Demonstrate the faith
that you have in their capacity now and how it will increase
in the future.

4. *Elevate and reward A-players.* Place A-players in pivotal positions as well as provide them with financial compensation commensurate with these positions. More than
anything else you can do, this action demonstrates how much
you value personal change capacity; it will create excitement
and energy around this concept. It will also demonstrate that
the traditional ways in which people moved up in the organization—performance reviews, seniority, and other methods—
now take a backseat to change capacity.

Be forewarned, however, that you may find some stumbling blocks to elevating and rewarding A-players. In one large pharmaceutical company, Linda, a vice president, wanted to place Don, an A-player, in charge of a team that was going to open a new, state-of-the-art manufacturing facility in Asia. When she told her boss of her plans, she was met with resistance. Why was she passing over Martin, who had more experience and more years with the company than Don? Not only that, but Linda wanted to give Don a significant salary increase, and her boss was even more resistant to this notion, telling her that she was "breaking the rules."

Recognize that you may have to break some rules to elevate and reward your A-players. You may be bypassing the traditional rewards and recognitions systems in your organization, which have been broken for years and in many organizations need to be blown away. Linda was able to bypass them because her boss's boss was a sponsor of the change capacity assessment she and others in the organization were conducting, and she received support from him for her actions. If you don't have similar support, you may have to bend the rules rather than break them, justifying your moves by enlisting the support of sympathetic bosses and HR people. If you are in HR, this is the action most deserving of your support. Because you understand the rewards and recognitions system better than most, you should be sufficiently savvy to come up with a plan to elevate and reward A-players. You may want to rely on documented evidence of personal change capacity results, since this "hard" data makes a powerful argument to place A-players in key positions. If your organization is embarking on a major change strategy, management is usually relatively open to ideas that will facilitate implementation of that strategy.

Communicate about Change

Communication means much more than CEO pronouncements about how the organization needs to change or general guidelines about how it will change. In both your formal and informal conversations with your people, as well as in written and electronic correspondence, help people locate themselves on the change continuum: where they are, where they've been, and where they're going.

Too often, people in changing organizations are confused about the change strategy and their role in it. They lack the information necessary for them to understand why the organization is changing and what their group and they as individuals need to do to make change happen. You can do a number of things to communicate this information properly, as shown in Figure 7-1.[2]

In the change communications process shown in Figure 7-1, the burning platform provides the "push" while the destination is the "pull." You can't expect people to embrace a development plan only because they understand the compelling reason why the company must transform itself without knowing where this transformation is going to lead (or vice versa). Similarly, it helps people orient themselves when they know where they are in the change plan and what they've accomplished toward achieving change goals.

Figure 7-1. Mapping Strategies: Change Communications

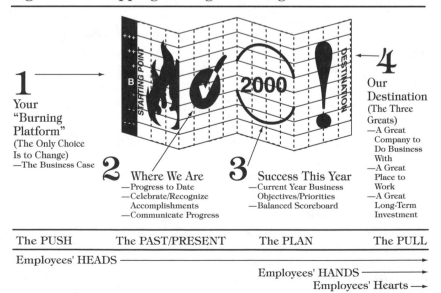

1			**4**
Your "Burning Platform" (The Only Choice Is to Change) —The Business Case	**2** Where We Are —Progress to Date —Celebrate/Recognize Accomplishments —Communicate Progress	**3** Success This Year —Current Year Business Objectives/Priorities —Balanced Scoreboard	Our Destination (The Three Greats) —A Great Company to Do Business With —A Great Place to Work —A Great Long-Term Investment
The PUSH	The PAST/PRESENT	The PLAN	The PULL

Employees' HEADS ────────────────────────────────→
                    Employees' HANDS ──────────→
                        Employees' Hearts ──→

Be prepared to share information with your group that you may not have shared in the past. Companies tend to be somewhat secretive with their change strategies and are paranoid about word leaking out about how they intend to transform themselves. While there may be competitive reasons to keep some strategies and tactics secret, the majority of information should be freely dispensed.

Let's focus on the two key areas of information—the burning platform and destination—and how to communicate them effectively.

Identify Your "Burning Platform" for Change

The term "burning platform" derives from a Ted Koppel story on *Nightline* in which Koppel was interviewing a worker who had just escaped from a burning oil platform in the North Sea. In his erudite way, Koppel told the worker that it was very courageous for him to jump off the derrick into a sea with burning oil slicks. The worker replied in words to this effect: "Hell, it wasn't courageous; I had no choice."

You want to communicate to your people what the burning platform is in your organization. Give them very detailed information about why your company has to downsize, merge, go global, revamp a process, or retool a plant. Explain why there is no alternative to whatever change strategy is being launched, and how it's imperative that the change strategy succeed. Don't sugarcoat the peril of the situation (if it's indeed perilous) or pretend that everything will turn out fine. The odds are your company wouldn't be making a significant change unless there was a major problem or it anticipated a major problem. It may also be that change has been catalyzed by a golden opportunity (though I find problems are the more common catalyst for change).

As you discuss this burning platform, explain why alternatives to the change strategy aren't feasible. Talk about why maintaining the status quo will result in disaster and why a scaled-down change strategy won't solve the problem. It may be that change calls for painful choices and difficult decisions; the company has to lay off people, close a plant, or relocate.

The change requires everyone to learn a new process or adjust to new policies. People need to be convinced that there is no other choice than the change program that's been laid out to them. From an HR perspective, communicate the people issues and how they can't be achieved without change. For instance, it may be that you've tried to reduce staff through early retirement offers and attrition (i.e., not filling vacated positions), but these measures haven't sufficed. Discuss what HR has done to meet objectives and why it hasn't been enough.

Identify the End-Goal of Change

At the same time, help everyone understand the destination in equally specific terms. Clarify how the changed company will be improved in three different ways—that is, how change will create:

▲ *A great company to do business with.* This is where you present the business case: how a given change will help the company gain a competitive edge. People are surprisingly interested in this information, even though they may be part of a large corporation and feel that a company's direction has little impact on their careers. It is important for most employees to realize that a change strategy isn't a harebrained scheme concocted by a showboating CEO but a well-thought-out strategy designed to increase an organization's power and presence in the marketplace.

▲ *A great place to work.* From a self-interest standpoint, people are most concerned about this area. How is a change strategy going to affect their career opportunities, help them develop marketable skills, and create a workplace that's both fun and meaningful? What work benefits will result as part of the change? Will it become easier to obtain needed resources? Are people going to be given more chances to make decisions and get their ideas heard?

▲ *A great long-term investment.* Because many employees now have a financial stake in the future of their organizations (through various benefit plans including equity ownership), they are naturally interested in how a change strategy will impact the company's fortunes. While this is a highly speculative subject, you should at least share the thinking of management about this issue. How will a given change impact a company five years down the road? Ten years? Even smaller-scale changes that are part of a larger change plan can be talked about in these terms.

In the feedback and development steps that follow (Chapters 8 and 9, respectively), you'll cascade down the burning platform and destination topics to a group and individual level. For now, the objective is simply to help people make sense of why they are going to be asked to do things differently and take on new or more assignments. All you need to do is hold frequent one-on-one and group discussions about these points, repeating your information in various ways. If you are a line manager, bring in HR professionals to share their perspective. If you are an HR staff member, bring in a manager. Written memos about burning platform and destination issues are also fine.

Repetition is important. I've found that change strategies invite all sorts of rumors and promote negative attitudes, and you can't counteract this effect by one formal announcement. Repetition helps drive home the points you need to make and lessens the chance of miscommunication.

Refocus on External Rather Than Internal Issues

In organization after organization, people resist growth and development plans because they seem irrelevant to their purposes. Typically, their purposes are internally focused, directed at in-house processes, policies, and people. Everyone gets caught up in how they are getting the work done rather than the ultimate purpose of that work.[3] Discussions are always about how to make the work easier to do, how to make systems function better technically, and how to deal with tension between two individuals or two groups. Outside of the sales department, discussions about how all this work affects the customer is relatively rare.

The customer—the external issue—needs to become your group's focus. If it isn't, your people may find it difficult to accept and embrace the development plan you present to each key member. The "why" behind most change—why they need to develop—will probably have much more to do with external rather than internal goals. If you are asking an information technology (IT) manager to design a completely new process that will ultimately give customers more information when they need it and that manager is thinking about how he can tweak the software so it will save a few minutes of downloading time each morning, he's not going to be receptive to the direction in which you want him developed.

One way or another, customers are the external focus of change strategies. Whether the change effort involves bringing in new technology, becoming a stronger global company, or creating new products and services, the ultimate goal is to serve the customer better, faster, and cheaper. While the initial goal might seem like it's purely internal—creating a new manufacturing process that will improve production efficiency— the end-goal is to manufacture products in ways that allow savings to be passed on to customers.

Talking to people about how their work affects the customer is an easy way to create an environment in which change-based development is accepted. Focus on how your particular group affects customers in four ways: why customers consider the company, why they choose the company, why they stay with the company, and why they leave the company. Help your key people explore what the group might do to attract, retain, and grow customers.

At one financial institution, these discussions had a galvanizing effect on how a wide range of people thought about their work. Sharing "privileged" customer information helped enormously to convey a sense of purpose to employees: For example, "More than two million customers closed accounts or left the bank in the previous year," and "A customer with two or more of the bank's products generates more than two times the net income as a single-product relationship." Armed with this information, people in diverse work groups—IT, HR, finance—stopped looking exclusively at how they could make their own jobs easier and began creating innovative ways of serving the customer better. By doing so, development around change issues was infinitely easier; the majority of key people understood why they were being asked to develop in new and different ways.

Create an Open, Flexible, Trusting Environment

Helping your people cope with change can be a daunting task. You have only so much time and money to spend on developing people in a direction congruent with your change mandate, and you want to be as efficient as possible. Creating a hospitable environment for development can facilitate this process.

Beyond the ways I've suggested so far for producing this environment, there are three simple things any manager or HR person can do to prime key personnel for feedback and development plans:

▲ *Be open to people's concerns.* You are going to be asking a lot of your people, and they are going to have questions they need answered before they'll respond positively. If you seem closed off or intimidating, they will be reluctant to broach any sensitive subject. Being a good, empathetic listener is a way to achieve a degree of openness. When someone asks you why changes need to be made since the company has been doing fine for years without them, don't bite the asker's head off. Try to understand the fear that underlies the question and address the source of that fear—job security.

▲ *Be flexible when it comes to both development and vertical and horizontal movement.* Your key people may come up with better ideas than you have to acquire targeted skills and increase their change response and versatility ratings. Listen to their suggestions. It may be that they know of a better training method than the one your company uses for a particular skill, or they'll recommend a coaching tool they want you to use to help them learn to take on roles of greater scope and scale. They may also have a better sense than you do of how they can effectively implement a piece of the change strategy; they may suggest a role for themselves that's ideally suited to their current talents.

▲ *Be trustworthy by talking honestly and straightfor-wardly.* This issue goes back to the earlier discussion about cultures of hope and accommodation. These cultures foster dishonesty and make it difficult for anyone to take what some-one says at face value. When you present your feedback and development plan to a key person, he has to believe implicitly what you are telling him. Any suspicion that you have a hid-den agenda will detract from his motivation to do what you request. By communicating clearly and honestly with your people about a variety of issues, you are demonstrating that you're someone they can trust. This trust will go a long way toward encouraging them to develop in change-directed ways.

You're not going to change who you are and how you've run your group overnight. If you are in HR, people will proba-bly already have preconceived notions about you. Ideally, you're already perceived as being open, flexible, and trustwor-thy. If not, making an effort in each of these three directions will serve you well as you start sharing assessment feedback with the people you're depending on to facilitate change.

8

Providing Feedback
That Facilitates Change
Agendas

First, to be effective, feedback about personal change capacity needs to communicate your team's conclusions about an individual's change responsiveness, versatility, towering strengths, challenges/unanswered questions, and development needs. Second, it should also give people an opportunity to provide you with their feelings about what you are telling them. Feedback is a misnomer in the sense that you're actually engaging in a dialogue. Third, it should impress upon them the role they need to play in making change happen, both in the short term and the long term.

Ultimately, the goal of these three feedback requirements is to energize and excite people about the role you need them to play and the development they need to go through. I've found that the pre-feedback step of creating the proper environment (Chapter 7) helps people to be much more receptive to the results of their change capacity assessments. Nonetheless, you'll find a wide range of reactions to feedback no matter what you do beforehand. On the negative side, denial, anger, and cynicism are possible reactions. But even generally positive reactions can be accompanied by misinterpretation.

It is therefore important to communicate feedback clearly, motivationally, and in a way that allows your people to ask questions. It's also important to schedule your feedback session as close as possible to your development session. In fact, I often combine feedback and development into a half-day meeting in which I provide an individual with feedback from the assessment and then explain our views about his development plan and how it flows from that feedback. For our purposes here, it's easier to discuss feedback and development separately.

As a general rule of thumb, if you come from a human resources (HR) background or have training as a coach, you will handle feedback more effectively. You've experienced the reactions of people who have been told they have trouble with change or need to change—reactions that range from denial to anger—and you've learned how to get the message across with maximum impact and minimal animosity. Without this training, you may want to consult with your HR group or bring in someone who can coach you.

Throughout this chapter, I'll share techniques about how to deliver feedback with development in mind. Before that, however, I'd like to warn you about the three most common mistakes people make when delivering personal change capacity feedback.

Errors That Destroy the Feedback Process

Perhaps the biggest mistake organizations make is to fail to give any feedback at all, going straight from assessment to development. This is more common when the individual being assessed is a higher-level manager. For some strange reason, companies are much better equipped to provide feedback to line workers than senior managers. Superior information systems and measures result in faster and more detailed feedback to line people. Higher up, not only are the measures and information systems inferior, but the pervasive attitude is that feedback is no longer necessary; that people can move forward, develop new skills, and assume more responsibility without a significant amount of feedback. As a result, some managers don't share the results of personal change capacity assessments with their direct reports, simply explaining that they need to do some work in areas X and Y, and that's why they've been enrolled in a given program.

Without feedback, people have great difficulty increasing their personal change capacity. They lack the self-awareness, knowledge, and motivation necessary to embrace development and change effectively. With feedback, personal change capacity is likely to improve, provided the following mistakes can be avoided:

1. *Assigning a change capacity grade.* Just because you've categorized your people as A-, B-, C-, and D-players (or red, yellow, or green according to a stoplight analysis) doesn't mean you have to share that information with them. The grades are for the benefit of you and your team, not for the individuals being assessed. There is nothing to be gained and much to lose if you reveal these grades. Invariably, some B-, C-, and D-players will protest the grade you gave them as being too low. Even worse, some people will accept your grade as irrevocable and damning and lose their incentive to improve their change capacity. All they hear and remember is the grade, no matter how many other positive things you tell them. It is even unwise to tell A-players how you've rated them. Not only will they share this information with other people who have been assessed (and those other people will feel badly if they also didn't receive an A rating), but they may assume that they have it made and that the high change capacity obviates the need for further development and growth.

2. *Treating a change capacity assessment like a perfor-mance appraisal.* Feedback from performance appraisals tend to be skewed toward the middle ground. Weaknesses are downplayed and strengths are shortchanged in order that no feelings are hurt and people all receive the same basic scores. You are essentially telling everyone they are C-players, with some C pluses and some C minuses. This type of feedback is worthless, especially when it comes to change capacity. You need to be honest and straightforward if you want the feedback to motivate employees to make the effort to improve their ca-pacity.

In addition, performance appraisals tend to focus on skills and results. People are rated on what they are good and not good at and how this translates into profitability and productivity. Sadly, organizations often undertake performance reviews primarily to justify salary adjustments. Change capacity runs on a different system of measures, one that is less tangible than that used to judge performance. You are not focusing on how people do their current jobs as much as how they've done their jobs in the past with regard to change and how they might handle change-based roles and responsibilities in the future. Therefore, it is a mistake to deliver feedback with the specificity of a performance appraisal. If you provide employees with tremendous detail about why you've rated them as a passive change responder or as having limited versatility, you're going to get bogged down in unresolvable arguments. While some detail is necessary, don't share everything your assessment team has discussed. In addition, explain that your assessment isn't fixed but eminently improvable. The development program is the key to improving people's change capacity, and if they improve, they will be given more responsibility for planning and implementing change.

3. *Delivering a monologue.* After you have shared your team's conclusions about personal change capacity, you want a certain amount of discussion and questions. It's productive for people to ask questions and even challenge your assessment. Remember, they haven't been allowed to participate in the assessment; they may have information or ideas that your team lacked. While it's doubtful that anything they say will affect how you've assessed them, it may affect how you plan to develop them. Individuals may have great ideas about how to improve their change capacity or put the assessment in a broader context (e.g., explaining why they had resisted change in a given situation). Monologues can be devastating for the individual and discourage development. Dialogues can allow people to express their feelings and clarify what you've told them. Even if people disagree with your assessment, they are much more likely to take what you've said seriously if they're allowed to communicate their disagreement. Instead of seeth-

ing inside about their rating, they can express their anger and move on.

What to Say and How to Say It

Now that you know what not to do, let's focus on what you should do to maximize the benefits of your assessment feedback.

First, you must convey five areas of information to the individual being assessed:

▲ Change response rating
▲ Versatility rating
▲ Challenges/unanswered questions
▲ Towering strengths
▲ Development needs

One of the easiest ways of conveying this information is by showing individuals the profiles you and your team have created for them (discussed in Chapter 3). These profiles are snapshots, and they allow you to give people a summary of their change capacity without going into great detail. Once people view their profiles, they will invariably have questions about their change response and versatility ratings. What you'll need to do is explain that change response is the team's assessment of their past reactions to change, and versatility is an assessment of their future ability to adapt and take on new or bigger roles and responsibilities. At this point, you'll need to provide some clarification about the ratings. Here is some appropriate feedback to offer based on each rating category:

Active Responder

▲ You've been one of our most valuable resources for leading change.
▲ Relatively few people in the group received this high of a rating.
▲ We expect a great deal from you in helping us plan, implement, and lead change efforts.

Passive Responder

▲ This is a solid rating.

▲ It's important to keep improving, and we think you can grow in this area.

▲ You can become an active responder, and your development plan is designed to help you achieve that goal.

Reactive Responder

▲ You make strong contributions when assignments are traditional and comfortable.

▲ You don't lead change and often respond apathetically or negatively when asked to do something new or different.

▲ We want you to play a larger role in the change process in this group, but first you need to develop in certain areas.

Blocked Responder

▲ You consistently react negatively when faced with anything that's new or different.

▲ There's a great sense of urgency around the need for you to improve your response to change.

▲ We've created a two-month to three-month improvement plan; if you don't meet these goals, we need to consider other alternatives (i.e., transfer, demotion, termination).

Clearly Versatile

▲ We believe you are sufficiently flexible to take on the new roles and responsibilities that come with change.

▲ We anticipate giving you a number of stretch assignments and leadership positions as we embark on our change strategy.

Expandable/Versatile

▲ You should be able to take on some new roles and responsibilities.

▲ We intend to give you major new assignments in specific areas related to our change effort.

Limited Versatility/Irreplaceable Pro

▲ We value your technical skills and intend to put them to good use as we change.
▲ You'll receive some additional responsibilities within your area of expertise, but going outside this area will require development.

Limited Versatility/Well-Placed

▲ We see you continuing in your present role.
▲ We would like you to take on new roles and responsibilities, but we don't anticipate this happening in the near future.

Minimally Versatile

▲ Your current role and responsibilities will probably diminish as we change.
▲ If you can't become more adaptable in your approach to our changing environment and demonstrate greater adaptability in the next few months, we will have to consider other alternatives.

In essence, delivering explanations of these ratings means walking a fine line between the general and the specific. You don't need to cite chapter and verse about each incident that went into the final rating; an example or two from your team's discussion will be sufficient. In most instances, use the most obvious, recent example of behavior that resulted in a given rating. Nor do you need to get into personalities and talk about what each member of the team said about a particular individual.

In terms of the other feedback information, towering strengths can usually be conveyed quickly and without much reaction from the individual. Development needs, too, don't require a long-winded explanation at this point since you'll be going into detail in the next step. Here the purpose is simply to break the ice by introducing a one-sentence description of what the need is.

Challenges/unanswered questions may require more time and discussion, and you may want to create a dialogue around this subject. (Later in this chapter, I'll examine the types of dialogues that are worthwhile during feedback sessions and how they can help answer unanswered questions.)

The final "comments" section of each individual's personal change profile provided you with a chance to include observations about other issues that might affect personal change capacity, such as change idiosyncrasies. You also should consider some of your conclusions formulated during the roadmap step (Chapter 6) regarding an individual's career management issues, problems with a boss, and so on. In most cases, however, these issues will be more important for an individual's development plan rather than for the feedback you provide. As a general rule of thumb, comments should be included in feedback only when there is a major question mark surrounding an individual's change capacity and you want to get the assessed individual's input on the subject. For instance, if Jerry is an active change responder and expandable/versatile in most situations but plunges to a blocked responder and limited versatility rating whenever he works on Tom's team, you might want to ask him for his opinion on why that is. You may learn something valuable not only about Jerry's personal change capacity but about Tom's as well.

Catalyzing Energized and Informed Responses

No matter if you are providing feedback to an A-player or a D-player, you should follow a relatively consistent format. While you're obviously going to send a different message to someone with a high change capacity compared to someone with a low rating, you can maximize the impact of that message if you deliver it in the following way:

1. *Begin with a general statement about what the change capacity assessment entailed and why it's important.* People

are going to be naturally curious about the assessment process, whether or not they've previously heard about it. They will want to know how it is different from the company's performance appraisal process, who did the assessment, and so on. While you shouldn't get bogged down in a detailed description of the process, you should share some general information about what the assessment entails. For instance:

> A team of managers has just completed a personal change capacity assessment of our key people. The point of this assessment is to ascertain who deals well with change and can take on a larger and more diverse workload as we move forward. It's also to determine how we can increase this change capacity through development. Our assessment is based on a number of factors, but the two main ones are change response and versatility—the former being how well someone has responded to change in the past and the latter being someone's ability to adapt to new roles and responsibilities in the future.

You don't have to say much more than this. It's fine if you want to explain who was on the assessment team or to fill people in on the other factors you'll be discussing with them. Simply satisfy their curiosity about what the assessment was about, then follow up with an explanation of why it is so meaningful to the organization and the individual and how the cumulative results (of all the people assessed) will help in the management of the company's human assets. Again, be brief. Talk about how it has become imperative that everyone learns to respond positively to new and unfamiliar circumstances and events because the company's future depends on it. Refer to a specific change strategy that needs to be implemented and use it as an example. Then, segue to the role that the individual needs to play to help make this strategy successful. Conclude by emphasizing that this is an ongoing process and that change capacity is something the individual and the organization need to work on not only in the short term but also in the long term.

2. *Provide a straightforward summary of the individual's change capacity assessment, starting with the general conclusion and moving to a specific example that illustrates this conclusion.* Straightforward is probably the most important word here. Don't get sidetracked by offering justifications for the assessment or providing mounds of evidence as if you were trying to win a court case. Neither should you turn the assessment into a personal attack: "We've told you before you need to be more flexible and this just proves our point!"

The brief examples given earlier of what to say and how to say it will help you know the messages you should send. Be as clear and concise as possible. For instance, Joe was a reactive responder who was also rated as a limited versatility/ irreplaceable pro. Joe was highly ambitious, and his boss anticipated a negative reaction when he shared the results of the assessment with him. Joe, in fact, had lost his temper over a mildly critical evaluation in a recent performance appraisal. But Joe's boss followed these guidelines and was especially good at conveying that despite Joe's technical proficiency, he was having trouble with anything that varied from the norm. Joe's boss cited a particularly telling example of Joe's fight against a corporate-mandated procedure that turned out to increase productivity significantly. Rather than protesting the assessment, Joe agreed it was fair and said he had never really thought about his change capacity before. By the end of the feedback session, Joe accepted that he needed to improve this capacity if he was going to fulfill his career ambitions.

3. *Discuss the role the organization sees for the individual in a changing environment and how the development plan is designed to help someone fulfill this role.* Again, deliver this message quickly. For instance:

> We want you to be a member of the new cross-functional team that's going to be set up for the Pan-Asian group, but that means we need you to take cultural awareness training since that's a

targeted skill but not your towering strength. As
a passive responder, you certainly don't fight
change and often support it well, but we want
to move you into the active responder range,
and we want to provide you with some additional coaching to get you to that point.

The combination of an exciting new role and the development plan to move someone into that role usually has a
motivational impact. For A-players and B-players, make this
linkage as clear as possible. For C-players and D-players, exciting new roles are probably off in the future. For them, communicate that improvement is expected, especially if D-players
want to continue in their current role.

4. *Engage in a dialogue about the feedback.* This is crucial for a number of reasons. First, the individual may help
you address a challenge/unanswered question by providing
information you lack. If your assessment team was worried
about someone's ability to handle a global assignment, bring it
up with her and see how she reacts. This is an opportunity for
the person to demonstrate that she's already gained experience
working globally at another organization or to talk about how
she intends to gain this experience.

Second, you want to give someone the chance to make
suggestions that will facilitate her development. I remember a
highly competent middle manager at a large corporation who
held the same manufacturing post for eleven years, and the
assessment team seriously doubted that she could handle a
much broader range of tasks. When told this during the feedback session, she suggested that part of the problem was that
she was so good at what she did that her old boss didn't want
her to do anything that would take time away from what she
did best. She suggested that she be given some "stretch" assignments that would allow her to take on new, unfamiliar
jobs.

Third, dialogue is a forum for people to express their own
ideas about their change capacity. While it's true a dialogue
can also turn into a forum for complaints, it more often is a

way for people to explore their feelings about change. Many times, they've never talked to anyone about their change capacity. They naturally have questions and concerns, and a dialogue allows them to talk out loud and arrive at their own conclusions about how they have responded to change and how they might approach new assignments in the future.

Troubleshooting Negative Responses

By and large, the majority of people assessed will react positively to new change-focused assignments and development plans. During the feedback session, they'll contribute ideas that will facilitate their development and ask good questions designed to clarify what you expect of them.

Others, however, will resist your feedback. They will do so for a variety of reasons: They don't understand the implications if they refuse to develop; they're risk averse (and don't want to try the new things you're suggesting); they're convinced they lack the ability to develop new skills, behaviors, and attitudes. Whatever the reason, you need to be prepared to deal with negative responses to feedback. Whereas A-players rarely are negative in these sessions, B-, C-, and D-players can be. Let's look at some of the most common negative reactions to feedback and the best ways to handle them:

▲ *Denial.* When you tell someone he's minimally versatile or a blocked responder, he tells you that he's excited about taking on new roles and he's always been open to change. If you inform him that your group requires people with good negotiating skills to make an acquisition work and this isn't his towering strength, he'll insist that he's always been considered a skilled negotiator. "Your assessment instrument is flawed," he might tell you, or "You probably just haven't talked to enough people about me."

Don't become enmeshed in a pointless "I'm right, you're wrong" debate. You can't win an argument with people in denial. Instead, focus the discussion on the need for development and the importance of this development to the individual and the group. Ideally, this person will leave the feedback meeting, reflect upon what you've said, and realize that if he wants to progress in the organization, he'll respond positively to the feedback. By avoiding a circular debate about what the employee did or didn't do, you give him space to reflect on his change capacity.

▲ *Anger.* Some people are distraught to hear that their change capacity needs improvement. I've found that some people become angry because they don't agree with the assessment; others are outright steaming because they feel the assessment is unfair in some way. ("No one ever told me that I'd be evaluated on my change capacity!" one irate manager once complained.)

It's fine to let people blow off a little steam during the feedback session, but too much anger becomes destructive when it prevents them from absorbing what you are trying to tell them. One of the best ways to defuse the tension in these situations is to emphasize that:

1. Change capacity is not fixed but can be improved through experience and development.
2. A low or moderate change capacity rating isn't automatically a black mark on the person's career record; it's simply a signal that a new area of competence must be mastered.
3. A low personal change capacity mark doesn't mean the person's not a valuable, productive employee. Technically competent people still have an important place in the organization, but if they want to assume positions of greater influence and responsibility, they need to improve their change capacity.

▲ *Skepticism/cynicism.* Invariably, feedback brings out some skeptics and cynics. They won't take the personal change capacity assessment seriously or they'll sneer at its relevance, viewing it as just another corporate fad. They may refer to another type of assessment that was done in the past, one that was quickly ignored and forgotten.

You need to impress upon them that change isn't going to go away, that your group (and the organization as a whole) is committed to improving its change capacity, and that HR will make resources available to develop people in change-friendly ways. While you may have communicated this information previously (as suggested in Chapter 7), you need to make this point more personally relevant during the individual feedback session. Communicate that in the future, the best jobs in your group are going to go to those with the highest personal change capacity. Explain that people are going to be selected for pivotal positions to implement the upcoming change strategy according to the factors discussed and their ability to develop in targeted ways. If necessary, offer negative sanctions, especially for D-players who need to shuck off their cynical exterior and start making dramatic improvements. Developing in ways that improve change capacity is serious business, and your feedback session should leave everyone with that impression.

The Most Common Questions

Before moving on to creating and communicating development plans, let's conclude with the questions that people most frequently ask when they receive personal change capacity feedback. While you are bound to hear a wide range of questions, you are likely to hear at least one of the following queries. After each question, I've provided some tips on how to reply in ways that facilitate development and change leadership.

> Why is my change response rating somewhat higher than my versatility rating (or vice versa)?

Explain the difference between past performance (change response) and future adaptability (versatility). An individual may be an active responder because he's always been an enthusiastic supporter of new programs and strategies, but he's not rated as clearly versatile because he demonstrates some reluctance to take on challenging leadership roles; the conclusion of the assessment team is that he may shy away from unfamiliar responsibilities in the future. It is also possible that someone appears ready and eager to take on expansive new roles but has had problems with certain types of changes in the past.

While change response and versatility ratings are usually in the same ballpark (I've never seen someone who is minimally versatile and an active responder, for instance), someone can be and often is higher rated at one than the other. As a result, the development focus is on the weaker area.

> If I improve my change capacity, will I receive
> the promotion/raise I want?

The problem here is that you don't want people to perceive change capacity improvement to be a one-time event or something with a singular objective. While it's fine to state in general terms that people who reach development goals and improve change capacity will benefit from both career and financial standpoints, don't make a definitive promise.

For one thing, change capacity assessments shouldn't be the only factor in determining if someone should receive a promotion or a raise. For another, measuring improvements in change capacity can be tricky. Ideally, you need to assemble the same assessment team, and that's not always possible. In addition, the team might not agree on the level of improvement.

To answer this question effectively, respond by saying that although you can't guarantee the raise or promotion, you can guarantee that the employee is increasing the odds of receiving it.

> You've identified my development need as ___;
> why is this so important?

This is a good question that you should answer clearly and specifically. Don't brush off this individual with vague responses about how the organization has deemed something to be an important competency or how the team determined that "this is what you have to do to increase your value to the company." Instead, link the need to specific requirements of change. For instance, if the need is for Joan to learn how to manage a diverse workforce, explain to Joan that the company plans on transferring in people from Asia and Europe to form a global team, and that Joan is targeted for a specific position on this team. Or you can communicate that top management has set a strategy that is going to require certain skills and knowledge to make this strategy work, and this is why a development direction has been set in a certain way.

> How is my change capacity compared with other people (on my team, in my department, throughout the company)?

Don't back off from this question. It's fair for people to want to know where they stand on this important issue. Therefore, be straight with your people. Be honest with the D-player and tell him that his change capacity is worse than most. Be honest with the A-player and tell him it's better than most. You want people with high change capacities to feel good about their ability to lead change; you want them to take pride in their superior performance in this area. At the same time, you need people with low or moderate change capacities to be motivated to improve, and establishing a healthy competition can serve as that motivation.

9

Choosing the Development Options That Best Suit the Individual

Development usually takes place around skills. I'm suggesting that it should take place around change capacity instead. It's not that skill development is irrelevant to change capacity; it may be that an A-player needs to develop a towering strength that lines up with a targeted skill or that a skill set is essential for leaders to develop as part of an overall strategy. But this book's particular focus is on helping people develop in relation to their change capacity assessment so that they can function more effectively in a change-intensive environment.

After you have created the right environment and provided the right feedback, you are ready to develop people in ways that are somewhat different from how the process worked in the past. Not only are you focusing more on change capacity than skills, but you are also using different techniques as well as criteria for selecting which employees should be developed. Let's start out by examining these criteria so that you can use your development resources effectively.

Prioritizing Group Needs

Ideally, you'll possess the time and money to develop every key person you have assessed. Realistically, you'll probably have to make some choices based on available resources. You may only have the time and money available to develop one person into someone who can play a crucial role on your team. Although you may want to address the development needs of Steve, Sue, and Maria, your team is being asked to help the company outsource a major in-house function two months from now, and your group change capacity analysis revealed that the team is lacking A-players to lead the effort. Maria, however, is a strong B-player with the right towering strength (she's helped make the transition from in-house to outsourcing before), and you believe the team will be successful if it has an A-player to lead it.

Therefore, you can prioritize development based on your group change capacity assessment as well as by matching the targeted skills of an upcoming change effort with the towering strengths of the people in your group. Many times, however, you will want to develop people for more than one specific change strategy, or you may be responsible for a large group (e.g., an entire division or the entire company). When human resources (HR) is leading the assessment of a given group, HR may be operating under a corporate mandate of increasing the overall change capacity of its top people or managers in a particular function. No matter what the mandate, you are going to have to make choices—not only about which individuals should be developed, but also who is to be developed first.

ABC Criteria

The simple way of making these choices is to combine the results of your group with personal change capacity assessments. The group change capacity assessment will help you identify your group's readiness to make change happen; the personal change capacity assessments identify the people who are most capable of leading that change. Let's say that your change capacity matrix reveals that of the key people assessed, your group has ten A-players, fifteen B-players, seven C-players, and five D-players. This is a good mix and suggests that the group has plenty of candidates for change leadership positions as well as solid support people. The A's and some of the B-players should receive the bulk of the development work if your resources are limited. The odds are, however, that you'll still need to prioritize development for this group. To do so, use the following ABC criteria:

▲ *A-players with the highest change response and versatility ratings receive the most development attention.* This is very different from traditional development priorities, where the people with the most serious problems receive the bulk of the development focus. HR professionals often complain—with some justification—that the vast majority of their efforts are devoted to dealing with problem people. In change-based development, however, A-players will yield the highest development return because they are the ones who will assume pivotal positions and drive the change forward. They are the ones who will not only demonstrate leadership and initiative in making change happen, but they'll take on new and unfamiliar responsibilities to ensure change does happen. Sometimes A-players are ignored in development planning because it's falsely assumed that they don't need any or much development. While they don't need as much development as B-, C-, and D-players, there is always room to improve change capacity.

▲ *B-players—those you are counting on to move up to A-player status—should be the second priority.* It may that you have few (if any) A-players; therefore, you need to help B-players move up a level in terms of change capacity. It may be that you have some time before you need them to play a key role and can develop them over a period of a year or two. Or it may be that these B-players are on the cusp and you believe that development can quickly nudge them up a grade.

▲ *C-players who are irreplaceable pros are third on the list.* C-players usually possess towering strengths that you deem essential—they match your list of targeted skills—but you foresee these individuals as having difficulty in a volatile, changing environment. Your goal may simply be to improve their change capacity a bit in the short term so that they demonstrate some change responsiveness and versatility as a new process, system, or culture evolves. Or it may be that you think they have the potential to become B-players or even A-players given the right development plan.

As for D-players, make development decisions about them with your head and not your heart. If you haven't moved them down or out during the first step of this development phase, if you truly feel they will be able to improve their change capacity, and if you have sufficient resources, try to develop them. That's a lot of ifs, so you need to be careful that your sentiment doesn't sway your judgment. I've seen more than one manager who has decided to give a long-term employee a "last chance" via development. Humanistic HR staff sometimes encourage pragmatic managers to cut D-players some slack—to send them through a special program or bring in a coach to help them. There are some people, however, who are forever going to be inflexible and unresponsive to change, and if your team assessment has made this apparent, don't waste time trying to turn these individuals into something they're not. They may well be able to develop new skills but will never embrace, support, and drive change.

The other issue relates to whether your development is geared toward a short-term or long-term need. It's one thing to develop people so that they are capable of handling new roles and responsibilities for a strategy that has to be implemented next month. It's something else to develop them because your organization is changing, and you want to develop people in ways that will correspond to a five-year plan's goals. In the former instance, if your group change capacity reveals a preponderance of C-players and D-players, you don't have time for development and need to look outside the organization for solutions. In the latter case, you may want to develop those people (probably the C-players) who you believe have the best chance of improving change capacity over time.

Change Capacity Isn't Developed in a Classroom

The default option in most development plans is training. HR departments in many organizations have constructed elaborate training courses and structures (sometimes in the form of in-house universities) to help people develop in the proper directions. They also send their people—especially their executives—to outside programs to acquire targeted skills, behaviors, and attitudes. This works fine when the goal is to acquire technical/functional skills or even when trying to help managers become better listeners and negotiators. Developing change capacity, however, often requires other methods.

The following is a listing of different change capacity development methods, ranked according to their return on investment (with 1 being the highest return and 7 the lowest):[1]

1. Job changes
2. Job restructuring
3. Development-in-place experiences
4. Ongoing feedback
5. Learning from others
6. Motivated self-development
7. Courses

This ranking doesn't mean that courses are a useless change capacity development tool. If a targeted skill is time management and an A-player lacks this as a towering strength, classroom work might be called for. Similarly, if an unanswered question surrounding a B-player relates to his ability to manage conflict and confront others, then he may benefit from a training course.

However, you can't rely on courses for two reasons. First, changing environments makes it difficult for people to use these skills effectively. Although people may be able to manage conflict in a calm, unpressured climate, they may find it much more difficult to do so in a volatile, rapidly changing situation. Second, and perhaps more important, is that versatility and change responsiveness develop largely in real-time, real-life situations. Learning by doing is the best way for people to learn new ways of reacting to change and to take on new roles of greater scope and scale. Change capacity is an internal quality, and as such it requires the force of experience to reach it. Classroom learning is a more surface experience that may lack sufficient impact to transform people's attitudes and behaviors.

Let's look at the seven development techniques and how you might use them to develop your people.

Job Changes

This is primarily a development technique geared toward A-players, and it usually is designed to prepare them for pivotal change positions. For instance, Mark is an HR professional ranked versatile/expandable and an active responder. His organization wanted to promote him to an executive vice president position where he would be responsible for restructuring the entire HR department. Looking over Mark's change capability profile and the development conclusions noted in the roadmap step, Mark's boss (the company's CEO) decided that moving Mark to a new job would be the key to his development. A theme that ran through all the assessments was that Mark was somewhat reluctant to take on challenging assignments where he didn't consider himself an expert. This was why the assessment team placed him in the expandable rather than clearly versatile category; it was why his development need was specified as "taking leadership and managerial risks in areas outside of selection and succession"; it was why the roadmap development profile included a mention of Mark's idiosyncrasy of "driving change only when he feels in control of most aspects of what he's changing."

The new job was in the company's recently acquired London office, and though it involved HR responsibilities for that office, it also was broader in scope and scale than Mark's current job because it dealt with different compensations systems than he was used to. In addition, there were broader and more numerous hiring responsibilities.

Scope and scale are the two key factors to consider when using job change as a development tool.[2] They provide people with a chance to stretch themselves both in terms of the size of assignments as well as the type of assignments they undertake. In addition, it's important that the position place an individual in an unfamiliar setting; this gives the employee the opportunity to push the boundaries of change responsiveness (and as an active responder, Mark was capable of handling a doubly unfamiliar situation—a new country and a new position).

Job Restructuring

This is a development option to consider if an assessment reveals that an A-player or B-player must improve change capacity relatively quickly. The former option of job change requires time; it also requires a degree of commitment to an individual that is usually made only when a pivotal position is involved. Job restructuring can be implemented quickly and without major political or resource hassles.

While job restructuring can take many forms, it usually involves one of the following directions:[3]

▲ Redefining a job's area of responsibilities so that the individual must handle more tasks than before
▲ Redefining a job's area of responsibilities so that the individual must handle a new type of task
▲ Broadening a job's skill set so that the individual receives the opportunity to develop a towering strength that corresponds to a targeted skill
▲ Focusing job responsibilities on a specific project in order to answer unanswered questions or foster intensive learning to meet an identified development need

While restructuring a job isn't as radical a development tactic as a job change, it can provide quick, incremental improvements in change capacity. This technique can be used in a very targeted manner. If you have a B-player who you want to assume the task of supporting an A-player in reviving a slumbering unit of the company, you might want to stretch him in this direction by adding responsibilities for a product line that's been in the doldrums for years.

Development-in-Place Experiences

While this method can be used for A-, B-, and C-players, it is most effective in the following two circumstances:

▲ When people occupy pivotal positions and development is designed as a "test" to determine whether they can still be effective in those positions as their roles and responsibilities are expanded

▲ When people have better change response ratings than versatility ones, yet the major development issue isn't so much how they have dealt with change in the past but their potential for handling more difficult and unfamiliar assignments

What makes development-in-place experiences so effective is that they allow people to stretch themselves in familiar and comfortable environments.[4] While job change and job restructuring can have a greater impact on change capacity, development-in-place can be used more tactically. It is useful for zeroing in on a specific development problem or concern. It is also the easiest of the three techniques to implement, requiring no dislocation and few (if any) additional resources.

A traditional development plan would send people in these situations through various training programs. The person who needs to become more versatile might be assigned to a classroom course targeting new management skills. Someone in a pivotal position might be sent through an outside executive development program; such a program would be viewed as insurance against this person failing in a key position.

There's nothing wrong with these traditional training methods, but you might want to combine them with the development-in-place approach. Providing your people with opportunity to apply what they learn in the classroom will have a greater impact on their change capacity. While you can lecture people all you want about the importance of taking on more roles and responsibilities (and teach them time management skills that explain how they might manage those responsibilities), they also need to risk being more versatile before they adopt new behaviors. Therefore, add actual job responsibilities that correspond to the training someone is receiving.

Ongoing Feedback

This is an effective supplemental technique to the three previously discussed. While you give people feedback about their change capacity assessments at the start of the development process, ongoing feedback is designed to maintain the focus on change capacity improvement. In other words, you need to keep reinforcing your initial assessment and help people monitor the progress they are making in meeting change capacity goals.

There are literally scores of ways to deliver feedback, but the one most in vogue is the 360-degree approach. Receiving feedback from numerous and multiple sources (e.g., the boss, subordinates, peers, the boss's boss, and customers) can be an eye-opening experience for someone accustomed only to feedback from a boss. From a change capacity perspective, it can deliver the wake up call needed to help someone develop greater versatility and change responsiveness.

Ongoing feedback is not the panacea some in the HR training and development community believe it to be, however. That is, 360-degree feedback alone won't increase change capacity. It certainly won't turn a C-player into a B-player. What it will do is combine well with one of the more action-oriented development methods. By keeping employees abreast of how they are dealing with a job change or in a restructured job, you are offering your people an instrument to gauge their progress. People will feel more comfortable taking on a new task or take the risk of responding enthusiastically to a new process if they know where they stand. Simply by giving them input on how they're doing—good or bad—will help them get their bearings and know if they are becoming more versatile or change responsive relative to a specific assignment. Negative feedback can alert (and alarm) an individual that his change capacity is static. Positive feedback—the soft rewards of the boss saying that a job was well done—can provide a strong incentive to develop this capacity.[5]

I'm not particularly concerned about the form feedback takes. It's fine to experiment with a gamut of methods, from pencil-and-paper instruments to one-on-one sessions with customers to comparative feedback (i.e., How is your change capacity compared with that of someone else in the group?). The only caution I would issue is this: There is such a thing as too much feedback. If you overwhelm someone with information about her change capacity—if there are too many people providing too much data too frequently—she's going to react negatively. You want your feedback to serve as signposts along the way to improvement, not as ubiquitous, irritating billboards.

Learning from Others

For this development method to succeed, you must first tackle this question:

> Who can serve as a model for a particular type
> of change capacity development?[6]

In other words, if you want someone to move from being a B-player to an A-player, who else has recently made this transition? If a development plan is focused on helping Mark address an unanswered question or deal with a personal change idiosyncrasy, who else has dealt with that question or overcome that idiosyncrasy? If development is concentrating on improving change responsiveness, who else has improved in this area?

The idea is to create a perfect match—to allow an individual to observe, talk to, and learn from a person who has been there before. In reality, your group may not be sufficiently large to make this perfect match (at least the odds are against it) and you may not have the opportunity to find the right person outside your group. In these situations, you just need to locate an individual who has something in common with the person you are developing.

The easiest way to proceed is to look for someone who had to make similar improvements in change responsiveness or versatility (or both). At the very least, you are looking for a person who can serve as a development "model" and will be able to offer advice about what he went through and the steps he took to increase his change capacity. From the individual's perspective, just having someone to talk to who did what you're attempting to achieve makes development seem more doable. HR departments often are well aware of these models and can recommend someone who might facilitate the learning process.

Learning from others can be implemented in different ways. You can have someone observe the model in action, as if to say, "This is what an active change responder looks and acts like as he's leading a team into new territory." Interviewing assignments are also effective; they offer people the chance to ask others how they developed strength in a targeted skill or how they went from being passively accepting of change to driving it. You can also set up a more formal mentoring program in which someone is temporarily assigned to a mentor who can serve as a development guide. This last option usually is chosen when someone is viewed as having great change capacity potential or when the employee is being counted on to play a pivotal role in a specific change strategy. Because mentoring requires a significant amount of time—both on the part of the mentor and mentee—it shouldn't be used for everyone.

Motivated Self-Development

Ideally, everyone would be responsible for implementing his own change capacity development program. This would not only save time and money, but it would be an ongoing process of continuous development. Unfortunately, some people won't self-develop, no matter how much motivation is provided. While it is possible that people can acquire a new skill or adjust a behavior on their own, change capacity usually requires a more structured path. Most people need a formal set of measures and feedback offered by a new job assignment or set of tasks; they need the guidance and monitoring that comes with a supervised development plan.

Motivated self-development, therefore, should be geared more toward those individuals you are convinced are eager to develop in the ways you've outlined in your initial feedback session. Typically, these are A-players and some B-players. I should note, however, that A-players and B-players aren't universally able or willing to self-develop. For instance, passive responders by definition are not likely to show a tremendous amount of initiative.

Perhaps the best way this technique can be implemented is as an adjunct to one of the more formal development methods. I've found that motivated self-development can significantly increase the efficacy of classroom training, allowing people to put new knowledge and skills into practice. If, for instance, someone is taking a leadership training course, you might set up a motivational system that encourages the employee to demonstrate more leadership on the job. This can be as simple as sitting down with the employee and telling her that she's likely to receive more career opportunities if she expands her leadership roles and responsibilities in the next six months. While you can also set up a more formal motivational program—designating tangible rewards if the employee achieves certain goals—this tends to take much of the "self" out of self-development.

Some companies have had considerable success with motivational self-development, most notably Bank of America. Its self-directed development program is based on the premise that only those people who are aware of their improvement opportunities and take responsibility for seizing those opportunities will develop increased capabilities. This premise makes a great deal of sense; you want to impress upon your people the need for them to improve change capacity and that they ultimately bear responsibility for doing so.

My only quarrel with this concept is when it leads to unstructured, unsupervised development. Most people won't improve their change capacity significantly if left to their own devices. Therefore, emphasize the importance of self-development, but stay involved by measuring and monitoring development and providing feedback.

Courses

Courses are a standard development tool, and even though they offer the lowest return on development investment, they still can be a worthwhile investment. When skills critical to a specific change strategy are required or a change-related question must be answered by reinforcing a particular competency (e.g., Can Mary lead the new cross-functional group as well as she led her functional one?), classroom training is fine. In most instances, however, it's insufficient by itself. Coupled with one or more of the other six development techniques, traditional classroom training has a greater impact on change capacity goals.

If you are an HR person, you may reflexively want to rely on classroom training more heavily than other managers. If you've helped design courses and seen how they've benefited people in your company, you may not like the fact that I'm placing them seventh (and last) on my list of effective development techniques. Nonetheless, I've never seen a course—in and of itself—that significantly increased an individual's change capacity.

Creating the Development Plan

Once you have prioritized which employees should be developed first, you should create a written plan that clearly communicates to each individual what the development needs are, what development techniques have been chosen, and how development progress will be evaluated. To a certain extent, you've already set the stage for this plan in the roadmap step detailed in Chapter 6. Based on an individual's change capacity assessment, you created a general direction for development efforts. Now you need to provide more specificity to that direction.[7]

I don't believe in a rigid development plan structure; you should feel free to write the plan in a way that you think will be most effective. Even if you are an HR professional, you shouldn't feel you have to follow your function's development plan guidelines. What I would recommend, however, is being clear and concise. The following are guidelines for creating the three sections of the plan:

▲ *Development needs.* You want to create a summary of what you discussed during your feedback session with the individual, and you should refer to the change capacity profile on which the feedback was based. The key is stating each development need clearly and in ways that reinforce your verbal communication with this person.

▲ *Development recommendations.* Go through the list of seven development methods and choose the ones that fit the individual. You may choose to focus on one specific method or suggest a number of options, discussing the options with the person and getting his input on what makes sense to him. Choosing the right change capacity development tool involves a certain amount of guesswork. The guidelines I listed previously will help you make decisions, but sometimes it's difficult to know what will work best. Listing different options and talking them over with the individual may be a way to encourage the employee's responsibility for his own development and secure more of a buy-in for the methods chosen. In your description of each development method, be sure and tie it back to why it's important relative to the company's change strategies and situations.

▲ *Evaluation.* You must make sure everyone is on the same page about how development will be measured. You want to be clear that everyone will be held accountable for developing their change capacity, and putting the measures in writing is a good way to get this message across.

Developing Sharon Star

If you'll recall, Sharon Star was the A-player profiled in Chapter 3. As her profile indicates (see Figure 9-1), her versatility is superior; she can adapt and take on new roles and responsibilities with ease. She has an active change response rating and has demonstrated that she deals well with change in most situations.

Sharon's development is crucial to her organization on both a short-term and long-term basis. Long-term, Sharon is seen as a leader, someone who can help transform the company as markets change and new sales and distribution methods become critical. Short-term, Sharon is being considered for a pivotal position in a strategy to turn around a company the organization is about to acquire.

Let's examine the three-part development plan created for Sharon to help her improve her change capacity to the point that she can provide the organization with the change leadership it requires from her.

Sharon's Three-Part Personal Development Plan

Development Needs

▲ You must demonstrate an ability to lead a turnaround effort. The company is making significant changes in a number of areas in an effort to boost productivity and sales. Your high change capacity and towering strengths make you a good candidate to lead these turnarounds. But you've never managed a turnaround effort before, and the company must help you gain experience and expertise in this area.

▲ You have trouble working with and leading new people. You become uncertain and conservative when new people are assigned to your group; you need to become more adept at leading fresh talent, not just veteran talent.

Development Recommendations

▲ *Job restructuring.* Starting (name time frame or implementation date), you will join the acquisition team and de-

Figure 9-1. Personal Change Profile: Sharon Star

Confidential

Name: Sharon Star   Service: 8 (yrs)

Location: Los Angeles, CA   Title: VP, Supply Chain

Reports to: Amy Bishop   Division: _____

Years in Job: 1.5   Position Code: _____

Change Response:
Active

Versatility:
Clearly Versatile

Significant Towering Strengths	Key Development Needs
▲ Strategic Thinking —Sees patterns —Looks for opportunities and continuous improvement	▲ Sizing Up People —Needs more accuracy and to be more cautious with early read
▲ Execution Skills —Has track record of results in tough situations —Delivers results on a timely basis	▲ Strategic Agility —Can overdo her strength —Needs to be more patient with tactical or less competent people
▲ Leadership Skills —Attracts talent —Solid in her development of people	

Key Questions/Challenges

▲ Can Sharon provide leadership in a turnaround situation? She has not been involved in this situation, to date, but with the planned acquisitions downstream, this skill will be important. She needs to be tested here.

▲ Can Sharon quickly produce strong results with the new aggressive program that ties supply chain to the sales and marketing effort in the Seattle area?

▲ Can Sharon move up quickly without development? The organization doesn't need to put a talent like this at risk.

Comments

Make sure that we keep the three unanswered questions in the forefront. If we do move her up quickly, we need to ensure that she has a solid, experienced coach to work with her. She is very marketable, and while she's pleased with her job right now, we need to aggressively manage her compensation. She merits discussion every three months and needs to be given visibility.

velop strategies for assessing potential acquisitions and developing strategies to boost revenues and reduce costs for these acquisition candidates. You'll be asked to take on three new people to help pick up the slack as she focuses on the acquisition team work. Your focus in the former instance will be on developing leadership turnaround skills, and in the latter developing increased change responsiveness when supervising new people.

▲ *Learning from others.* You must work closely with David Green, who has extensive experience with turnaround situations and is also on the acquisition team. He has agreed to schedule time with you once a week for the next month to answer your questions and provide feedback about your work on turnarounds. Also, you must schedule time with Marcia Coll in HR (see next development recommendation).

▲ *Motivated self-development.* You should keep a journal of your interactions with each of the three people assigned to your group. Monitor your objectivity in assessing their efforts and your willingness to give them additional responsibilities if they perform well. Share your journal entries with Marcia Coll and solicit her feedback about how you are managing these new people.

Evaluation

1. Objectives

▲ Receive positive evaluations from David and Marcia based on your turnaround leadership skills and change responsiveness with new people

▲ Demonstrate an ability to obtain solid contributions from the three new people in your group and make valuable contributions to the acquisition team

2. Monitoring methods

▲ David and Marcia will provide written evaluations.

▲ You'll receive verbal feedback from three new people as well as other members of acquisition team.

Development Plan Variations

The focus of a development plan should be shaped by employees' change capacity profiles, group change capacity assessment, and targeted skill and pivotal position requirements. Situationally, you may need to develop a B-player into an A-player as fast as possible to meet a short-term group requirement. Or you may have the luxury of developing the change capacity of a number of people in the division over the next two years. Or you may need a plan to help someone in a pivotal position increase both change responsiveness and versatility rather than specific skills (e.g., the individual has all the right skills to lead a change strategy but lacks the change capacity).

Similarly, you're going to develop an employee such as Sharon Star differently from how you would develop your D-player, Ann Screen. With someone like Ann, you wouldn't want to invest in job change or job-restructuring methods; they would probably be wasted on her. Her development should revolve around feedback that jolts her—that helps her wake up to the fact that her change capacity is abysmal and that she needs to become more responsive and versatile if she wants to progress in the organization. Once she becomes aware of this need, the next step is some simple, motivated, self-development assignments that will test whether she is willing to increase her change capacity.

I've found that most managers and HR people can take the information contained in a change capacity profile and intuitively create an appropriate plan for that individual; it does not have to and shouldn't turn into a difficult task. Even if the plan isn't perfect, there's one more related step to the development process that usually helps keep people on the right track—coaching.

Coaching has become a necessary skill for every manager, and as Chapter 10 explains, a little coaching can go a long way toward helping people develop in productive change capacity directions.

10

Implementing Change-Focused Coaching Techniques

While coaching is sometimes listed under the "feedback" section of a development plan, I want to discuss it separately because it is so crucial for improving change capacity. There are all types of coaching approaches and theories, but my concern is the use of one-on-one coaching to increase change capacity. Development may require that someone become more change responsive or more versatile; it may be very specific about addressing an unanswered question, correcting a change idiosyncrasy, or working on a towering strength that matches a targeted skill. Development may also have the more generalized goal of moving someone from a B-player to an A-player.

As a result of these different objectives, coaching takes different forms. Some people need to be coached so that they become aware of how inflexible they are when it comes to taking on new roles and then take steps to become more versatile when asked to do what's new and different. Others simply need to be coached on strategy because it's a targeted skill necessary to achieve the group's change objective.

Unlike some other coaching approaches, change-directed coaching isn't a one-way street. Coaching has received a fair share of criticism—some of it deserved—for helping the individual but not the organization. The individual grows and develops, but the organization receives little, if any, benefit (especially if the individual becomes more marketable as a result of the coaching and leaves the company for another job). The coaching I'll discuss is value-added, resulting in employees who contribute more to the company because they are better equipped to lead and support change.

You may not feel you have the training or skills to be a good coach. While this is possible, what you do possess are unique insights about the change capacity of the people you've assessed. This knowledge is crucial for change capacity coaching, and it usually compensates for whatever natural skills or experience you lack. Later in this chapter, I'll talk about situations when it's wise to bring in another person to coach. For now, if you find coaching difficult or uncomfortable, rely on the human resources (HR) executive who was on your assessment team. If you are an HR professional who is skilled and experienced as a coach, you should volunteer to assist managers as they work with their people. I've found that if you simply make yourself available to answer their coaching questions or help them resolve particularly perplexing issues, you'll greatly enhance the process.

Perhaps the best way I can help you be an effective change capacity coach is by first explaining the four principles that should guide your efforts:

1. Start with the head-set issues.[1]
2. Facilitate learning.
3. Create influential people.
4. Encourage reflection.

Start with the Head-Set Issues

Let's say a development plan calls for restructuring an individual's job in order to test and grow her change responsiveness. For instance, Melinda's restructured job now requires her to work at a faster speed than in the past and with a process that is significantly different from the one she relied on before. As Melinda struggles to respond positively to her restructured job, she's going to need to test and develop new behaviors.

Before she can do that (actually, before she's willing to try a new approach), she needs to deal with the head-set issues. Specifically, why is it necessary to use a new process and work at a faster speed; what's the business context behind these changes? Coaching can help her address these issues.

In many work situations, managers lack the ability or inclination to deal with internal challenges. Some people manage through intimidation and don't feel the "why" needs to be explained. Others simply aren't aware of the importance of explaining the purpose, especially as it relates to change. Perhaps these attitudes were acceptable in the past, but today employees are not willing to accept things just because management says that's the way it is; they want to understand the big picture before they're willing to do something new or different.

For instance, Melinda's coach communicated clearly that the need for speed was the direct result of competitive pressures that made it imperative that Melinda and every manager in her functional group meet tighter deadlines. In fact, a number of customers had switched to competitors because of the company's slow response time. Not only was this the sort of information that Melinda, a midlevel manager, wasn't normally privy to, but it was delivered at exactly the right time. Melinda had complained to her coach about how difficult it was to meet her new deadline and suggested that in the rush to get things done quickly, quality might suffer. Her coach recognized that this was Melinda's reactive change response rating talking and that she simply didn't want to vary her routine. When he provided her with high-level information and shared with her a conversation he'd had with a top executive about the new process, Melinda was willing to look at what was being asked of her in a new light. Though she didn't instantly become a passive change responder—it took months to move her to that level—the coaching put her on the right track.

To get development off to a good start, help people understand the big picture in the following ways:

▲ *Intervene when employees begin to struggle with a change-focused assignment.* It doesn't matter what development tool you are using—they can be struggling with a classroom project, a job change, or a learning-from-others assignment. You want to start informing them about the "why" behind the change when they find themselves struggling or resisting. This is when they need and want help. By communicating the larger reason for a change, you can help someone clear this initial obstacle.

▲ *Share credibility-enhancing information.* When employees resist a new assignment or are reluctant to develop a new skill or behavior, don't coach them with a vague generality. For instance, don't say, "It's important that you adopt this new role because we're all taking on new roles." Instead, be specific and offer tangible reasons. Use studies that have been undertaken, conversations with top managers or consultants, and other inside information to give credence to the big picture you are drawing for them.

▲ *Show them the big picture.* Sometimes coaching opportunities aren't limited to telling. You may be able to let them look at a study your organization conducted. You may want to set up a meeting with your boss so that the individual can hear, from the horse's mouth, why he needs to take on additional responsibilities. Or you may want to let the individual observe a situation that graphically demonstrates the big picture: Let him sit in on a sales meeting with a customer and hear the customer complain about quality or missed deadlines.

Each of these coaching tactics facilitates a buy-in that makes it infinitely easier for someone to acquire the desired skills, behaviors, and attitudes.

Facilitate Learning

Increasing change capacity frequently relates to some type of learning. It may be as simple as learning a new skill that will help drive a particular change or as complex as learning how to be receptive to unfamiliar assignments and increased responsibilities. For an A-player, learning may revolve around a very specific and time-sensitive objective: Joan has to learn to be a better leader of teams in the next two months because the organization wants her to head the new cross-functional team it's launching. For a C-player, learning may be broad-based and gradual: Ned is an irreplaceable pro who has to learn how to open himself up to people and processes outside of his area of expertise, and his long-term development plan will help him achieve this goal.

One of the hot-button issues for coaches today is helping their people learn how to work in an increasingly complex and ambiguous environment. Many change capacity development plans will address this issue directly or indirectly. An unanswered question about a B-player might be whether he's able to manage effectively when he has to deal with paradoxical issues and resolve problems without clean, clear solutions. Or an A-player has not responded well in the past when confronting highly complex new assignments and has to learn how to lead amid difficult or complicated circumstances.

Coaches must look for learning opportunities and help their people take advantage of them. This can entail a number of coaching actions, including:

▲ *Intervening when the learning impulse becomes blocked.* Watch for signs of learning resistance. These signs range from outright refusal to do something that breaks with traditional practice ("I'm not going to do it this way; my way is better") to more subtle passive resistance (e.g., going through the motions of a development plan but lacking much enthusiasm or emotional energy). Intervening at these points simply means confronting an individual, pointing out what you've observed, and asking about this behavior. Many times, this action can help people become aware of an underlying resistance to change. Making individuals aware that their failure to learn is linked to their unwillingness to change can be eye-opening. They may rationalize why they aren't following through on the development plan in all sorts of ways, but a coach's intervention can help them see through these rationalizations and address the core issues: a lack of change responsiveness and/ or minimal versatility.

▲ *Identifying the best learning situations.* In your new role of change capacity coach, you need to keep an eye out for opportunities that will best address the change capacity issues identified in profiles and development plans. Plans that seem to address these issues effectively on paper may not work in practice. You need to be alert to situations where learning isn't taking place as well as emerging situations that might provide greater opportunities to increase change capacity. If classroom training isn't enabling someone to become more versatile, you might be aware of someone in the organization who can help this person learn how to take on new roles and responsibilities. Or you may find a way to restructure this person's job that is better suited to her learning needs.

▲ *Listening to people articulate what they've learned.* James was a B-player who was being developed so he could take over a key support position as his midsize organization restructured. As a financial director, he was being counted on by the functional head to help take apart their function and put it back together again. Unfortunately, James was reluctant to take on any type of operational role. He was strong with numbers, but his somewhat limited versatility, combined with his passive change response rating, caused him to shy away from anything that wasn't numbers-oriented. Yet James's towering strength—his financial acumen—would be of great value to his boss in the restructuring. Therefore, James's development plan called for him to rotate through a few jobs in the organization that would help him become more comfortable and skilled at nonfinancial tasks. His boss, who was coaching him, thought James was making good progress, but what really accelerated the learning process was a conversation James had with his boss in which he opened up about how difficult he found it to work in areas outside of his expertise. James's boss said very little in response, but his empathetic listening allowed James to work through some of the issues that were holding him back. After this session, James became much more willing to take risks with decisions outside the financial area.

Thus, make time to listen to the people you are coaching. Instead of playing the traditional role of boss where they listen to you, reverse roles and allow them to express their concerns and questions.

Create Influential People

A common goal in change capacity development plans is to help an individual segue from being a person of power to a person of influence. As organizations and their cultures evolve, there is a significant need for leaders to make this transition. Top executives realize that to fulfill their vision for the company—to help it run as a twenty-first-century rather than a twentieth-century company—they need influential leaders. These influencers are ideally suited to manage a diverse, young workforce that will not abide a military manager.

People with limited versatility have great difficulty mastering this new skill. Because influence is often a requirement for people assuming pivotal positions, it can be a serious obstacle in development.

If developing influence is a goal for the person you are coaching, you can do two things to help them achieve it. First, you can discuss with them why becoming a person of influence is important. This relates to an earlier point about helping everyone see the big picture. Sometimes people just don't get it: They're unable to relate a trait such as influence to specific goals for your group and the organization. If you can help them make this connection, they may be motivated to take the risks necessary to move from a command-and-control mentality to one of influence.

The other option is modeling influential behavior. If you, in your coaching role, tell a direct report, "Listen, if you don't stop using intimidation and start using influence to get things done, you're out of here," you can expect an unproductive reaction. If, however, you model influential behaviors both as a boss and a coach, then an individual will pick up on it. If you know of someone who is a better model, then let the person you are coaching observe that person in action. Sometimes people need to see how influence can work as a management tool before they start believing in it.

Encourage Reflection

One of the most challenging tasks for manager-coaches is giving someone the space he needs to reflect on his issues and actions. If you are accustomed to telling people to do something and seeing them respond immediately, you may find it uncomfortable giving them time just to think. Reflection actually is more than thinking. More precisely, it's a deeper form of thinking, one that allows people to contemplate important aspects of their work lives seriously and deeply.

Reflection is necessary because change is hard. Most people aren't going to increase their change capacity unless they really come to grips with current behaviors and attitudes and recognize the importance of adopting new ones. For someone who has spent years in a limited versatility, reactive change response mode, it's tough to leave that comfortable place and view change as a positive force and unfamiliar assignments as opportunities for growth. Reflection helps people roll this type of issue around in their minds. When you as a coach tell someone that she needs to think long and hard about why she fought against a new program or policy in the past, this catalyzes reevaluation and reformulation of beliefs, and ultimately it leads to testing of new behaviors. While reflection doesn't always work—sometimes an individual will not take the process seriously—it can help most people grasp a problem they are having while grappling with something new, different, or unfamiliar.

As a coach, you can encourage reflection in the following ways:

▲ *Ask people to take a moment and contemplate the most difficult change they've been asked to make in a work situation.* When they've thought of it, they don't have to tell you about it. Instead, ask them to think how they felt when they were asked to change—not what they thought about it, but what emotions were stirred up: anxiety, fear, anger, or uncertainty. When people are in touch with their feelings about a situation, it helps them reflect; they naturally wonder about why they were so fearful or angry.

▲ *Use a series of provocative questions that will force people to reflect on the problems they have with change.* For instance:

    ▲ When have you deliberately avoided taking on additional tasks because you thought it would be too much?

    ▲ Have you ever talked someone out of an assignment because it seemed to require skills or an approach that seemed beyond your grasp?

    ▲ What big question about your ability to lead/support change do you think exists in this company (or this team or department)?

    ▲ Why do you think you weren't ready to take on a pivotal position in a change strategy in the past?

▲ *Encourage reflection when people come to you upset and concerned with how their development plan is unfolding.* Your impulse may be to give them advice that helps them solve their problem. That's fine, as long as you first ask them to reflect on why they are encountering such difficulty implementing the plan. If you solve the problem right away, they won't think about it. What you want them to really think about is why a particular assignment or new responsibility is causing them such grief. Reflection may help them see that it's not the assignment per se that is the problem but their own internal response to change or unwillingness to be versatile.

I've found that some managers are dubious about the benefit of reflection in these coaching situations. They're often stuck in the old business paradigm where tools such as reflection were rejected as "soft" or ineffective. If you have an HR background or have had some exposure to psychology, you recognize that reflection is a catalyst for new behaviors; that changing the way we think and feel leads us to change the way we act. If you are dubious about this proposition, ask your HR group to provide you with some information about reflection or put you in touch with an outside expert.

Coaching Mistakes

Coaching to help people achieve change capacity improvements can be tricky. I've seen coaches veer away from the four principles just discussed and become ineffective or even counterproductive. Mistakes are common in this area, partly because coaching to improve change capacity is a relatively new endeavor; no one has much experience in doing it. In addition, the organization may have put someone in a position where it's difficult for anyone to coach him effectively. Let's examine some of these mistakes and how you can avoid them.

Mismatching the Coach and Employee

First, make sure the right coach is assigned to the right individual. As I emphasized earlier, most managers make good change capacity coaches of the people they've assessed. In some instances, however, you may feel you are not well-suited as a coach for a particular individual. In the most obvious case, the targeted skill/towering strength area isn't one in which you are an expert. You will be of little or no use to this person because you lack the knowledge and experience he needs.

An inappropriate coaching match also occurs when the coach lacks empathy for the change issue involved. For instance, Richard was extremely impatient with Judy, his direct report, because he was an active change responder who had always embraced change while Judy was a blocked responder who always ran from it (or even sabotaged it). Richard desperately wanted to help Judy become at least a reactive responder, and the long-term development plan gave him the time to achieve this goal. But Richard lacked the temperament to coach Judy effectively. When she'd come and talk to him about how difficult it was to adapt to the requirements of the new CEO, he would lose his temper and ask what was wrong with her. Richard was very poor at facilitating learning and encouraging reflection about change-related issues. While he might have done well at these tasks if he were coaching someone else, Judy's specific issues rendered him dysfunctional as a coach. Judy would have been better served by a coach who could empathize with change responsiveness struggle.

If you have doubts about your coaching appropriateness, consult HR. In some instances, HR has wisely recognized that a given manager lacks the empathy necessary to be a good coach or it has seen that the manager is struggling with helping an individual increase her change capacity. There are times when someone from HR takes over the coaching responsibilities. I've also seen HR bring in coaches from the outside, especially when the individual being coached is absolutely critical to the change effort (e.g., has or is being groomed for a pivotal position).

Inflating Expectations

Second, don't expect coaches to work miracles. As powerful a tool as coaching is, it is not going to do much good if the personal change capacity assessment and development plan are off target. Too many times, coaches shoulder the responsibility for helping an individual become a change leader or achieving some other dramatic transformation. If a C-player has been placed in a pivotal position that should be occupied by an A-player, no coach is going to be able to help that individual instantly become something he's not. The coach and the individual he's coaching are victims of wishful thinking.

I've worked for and consulted with organizations that placed unrealistic burdens on coaches; they're companies with cultures of hope and accommodation. In one instance, a company desperately wanted an irreplaceable pro with limited versatility to take on a huge new role in a recently acquired organization. This irreplaceable pro was a brilliant information technology (IT) professional, and the company needed him to use his IT expertise to revitalize the acquired company. This company knew that the IT executive was a reactive change responder and had limited versatility, but it hoped and prayed that the coach assigned to him would accelerate his development to the point that in three months, he'd be ready to take on a radically new assignment. The coach, of course, threw up his hands in frustration at the end of that time and told the CEO that it would probably take three years rather than three months for this individual to be ready to do what the company wanted.

Losing Organizational Focus

Third, don't coach as if the business doesn't exist. An amazingly common scenario is for a coach to work with someone on her *individual* development and lose sight of what the *organizational* goal of that development is. The coach will focus on helping Susan become more comfortable working in a rapidly changing workplace rather than helping her become a driver of change as her department becomes more reliant on outsourcing. Certainly the individual goal facilitates the organizational one, but if coaching is centered around Susan's individual, "psychological" issue, she may have difficulty translating that personal growth to business situations. A coach may help someone achieve an epiphany and become aware of a personal shortcoming related to change, but that's not enough.

The best coaches map the business terrain for their people. This means that they connect personal change capacity to group or company objectives and issues. They discuss the time constraints a team is under and why the team needs an individual to develop in a certain way in that time frame. They convey the business challenges the group is facing and how it needs an individual to step up to new and more varied challenges. They communicate how increased change capacity will give the group the additional A-player it needs to occupy a position pivotal to implementing a strategy.

Coaching a High-Potential, Low Change Capability Individual

Perhaps the biggest coaching challenge is someone who has the potential to contribute significantly to change efforts but who has underperformed in the past when faced with change. Bill Brightplus, one of the six people we profiled in Chapter 3, is an example of this type of employee.

As you might recall, Bill is a midlevel manager in his large corporation's financial group, a reactive change responder who is also in the versatile/expandable category. Bill has intelligence to burn, but he has also come close to burning some bridges because of his poor people skills. When his team has been asked to tackle a new or difficult project, or when there have been many new policies and procedures implemented, Bill has become resistant, ill-tempered, and dictatorial. At the same time, Bill is extraordinarily proficient from a technical standpoint. Not only is he skilled at the tasks related to his financial function, but he is an excellent strategist and has a clear vision of where the organization is heading. When Bill joined the company, he was tabbed as a future star. But over the years, Bill could be counted on to snap when he encounters an unexpected problem or when he's given a new, challenging assignment that requires a different approach. His periodic outbursts tends to take the form of alienating peers, subordinates, and superiors, as well as refusing to innovate.

The ambitious development plan created for Bill addresses these issues in a number of ways. However, Bill's boss, Mitch (the company's financial vice president), knows that coaching will play a big role in Bill's attempt to increase his change capacity. Mitch has taken on this role, not only because he knows Bill well and has the skills Bill lacks, but because he wants Bill to take on a recently vacated position in the finance group that will have broad and strategic responsibilities. Mitch's well-justified fear is that Bill will self-destruct in this position unless he becomes more change responsive and lives up to his versatility potential.

One of the first things Mitch did in the coaching sessions with Bill was to deal with the head-set issues. Bill's development plan mandated a job restructuring that gave him the opportunity to move outside his traditional role and take on a broader series of responsibilities. As Mitch had anticipated, Bill ran into problems almost from the start. Working on a cross-functional team for the first time, Bill blew up at team members who resisted his ideas. When Bill talked to his boss about what happened, Mitch took the discussion to a different level. He used it as a springboard to talk about big-picture issues. He explained to Bill that the company was changing and would continue to change; he shared a conversation he had recently had with the COO about the organization's five-year plan. He also made it clear to Bill that although the organization valued him and needed him to develop so that he could take on bigger and broader jobs, management was concerned that Bill had been so resistant to change in the past.

Then Mitch asked Bill to reflect on three possible scenarios. He said, "I want you to think about how your career in this company will turn out, and here are the three options available to you:

▲ Growing with the company and being a significant contributor to the company's evolution
▲ Making modest attempts at adapting and remaining in your current position in finance until retirement
▲ Staying exactly as you are and finding that the organization has given up on you"

This and other coaching approaches at least helped Bill become more aware of how his minimal change capability was hurting both the company and his career. Once Bill had that awareness, he was more open to coaching. During their coaching sessions, Mitch brought up two simple questions that he wanted Bill to address:

▲ Am I working at improving?
▲ How am I doing?

These questions proved pivotal because they provided Bill with tremendous opportunities to learn. Mitch routinely solicited feedback from Bill's cross-functional team about these two questions and shared their responses with Bill. This routine ensured that Bill would be highly conscious of his objectives. Perhaps more important, Mitch used these questions to help Bill articulate his feelings and measure his progress. At first, Bill admitted that it was difficult to improve his response to change; he was thrown off stride working with people in other functions who often knew more about the issues they were addressing than he did. At the same time, he talked about small steps he was making in the right direction—how instead of blowing up at a team member who challenged an assertion he made, he was able to take a deep breath, reconsider what he had said, and admit that perhaps he had been wrong. Feedback from the team confirmed that Bill was making small but important strides toward his development goals.

After a year, Bill was promoted to a broader, more strategic position within the finance group, and Mitch has every expectation that Bill will eventually become a change leader in the organization.

Let the Person You're Coaching Be Your Guide

Many well-intentioned coaches fail to solicit input from the people they are working with. They fail to do so because they're so intent on offering advice and providing direction that they don't make a consistent effort to draw out feelings and thoughts from people and incorporate what they hear into the coaching process. People can often reveal startling insights or provide information that helps coaches fine-tune a development plan and make it that much more effective. Because change capacity development so often has to do with internal issues, it's important to create a coaching dialogue rather than a monologue.

Here are some questions to ask of the individuals you're coaching:

▲ What progress did you make toward your development plan goals since we last met?
▲ What's getting in the way of your making progress?
▲ Is there anything I can do to clear away some of the obstacles? Are there resources you need me to obtain?

▲ Though you've made some progress so far, how do you intend to make more progress in the future?

▲ How are you responding to changes differently now than in the past?

▲ What specific efforts are you making to be more versatile? Are you taking on roles of greater scope and scale, and if so, what are they?

▲ Can I help arrange for you to try to take on new roles and responsibilities?

▲ Is there anything in the development plan that you're finding counterproductive? Is there a person or job assignment that you believe is hurting rather than helping your change capacity?

Development plans are rarely perfect, especially when they focus on something as intangible as change capacity. Ultimately, the coach must take responsibility for implementing them properly and adjusting them when they don't seem to be working, and the best way of doing this is by soliciting ideas and information from the people you are coaching.

Part Three

Organizational Readiness, Individual Action

11

Assessing the Organization's Capacity to Support and Facilitate Change

Up until this point, I've focused almost exclusively on the "people" component of change. My premise has been that successful organizational change begins at the individual level, and if the right people aren't in place to make change happen, then it won't happen. Most managers and organizations are unaware of their people's capacity for change, and as a result they go into a change program with their eyes closed.

I would be foolish, however, to maintain that successful change is singularly contingent on having the right people in the right jobs. Everything from technology to customers to time frames has an impact on whether change is carried out effectively. For this reason, it is important to assess these and other factors. This assessment is necessary whether you are the CEO attempting to transform the entire organization or a manager trying to implement your piece of a larger strategy. While this is not a book about how to formulate organizational strategies (there have been more than enough good books written on this topic), it is crucial to understand how to look at change holistically.[1] As you assess and develop your people to achieve a change-related objective, you must keep the big picture in mind.

Some of you will do so naturally. While training in personal change capacity assessment and development is virtually nonexistent, training in areas such as strategic planning is common. Still, even if you are a skilled strategic thinker, you may find it difficult to integrate that thinking with your personal change capacity assessments.

Before introducing the model that will help you assess the various organizational factors that will impact your ability to implement change successfully, let me emphasize that organizational assessment and development take place simultaneously with individual assessment and development. Although this issue appears near the end of this book, that doesn't mean it's the last thing you should do in the process. The recommendations made here and in the next chapter are relatively easy to do and can be carried out in tandem with your personal change capacity assessment and development efforts.

A Simple Model for a Complex Series of Factors

This change alignment model identifies four categories—strategy, people, process, and change implementation—to hold the diverse factors that you need to assess (Figure 11.1).[2] If they are in alignment, the fifth category—results—will be positive. Obviously these are broad categories, and just as obviously the more influence you have in a company, the more control you have over each category. If you are the CEO, it is within your sphere of influence to ensure that the change strategy is realistic, that change capacity assessments have been conducted, that processes support the desired changes, and that implementation is measured continuously and accurately.

But even if you are not the CEO, you can assess these factors to determine how they affect your particular area. While you may not be able to revamp a corporate strategy so it is aligned perfectly with what your group must accomplish, you can talk to your boss about where strategy is going off course and what might be done to correct it. I've found that human resources (HR) leaders, for instance, can exert great influence

Figure 11-1. Change Alignment Process

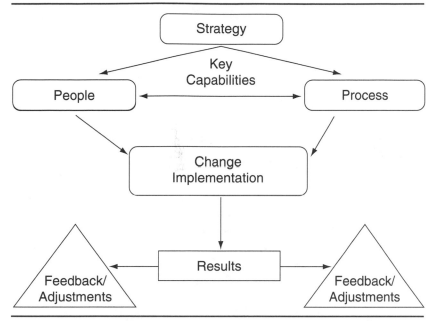

over organizational change capacity. Because of their roles within the organization, they are at ground zero for change capacity impact. If you are an HR professional, you know whether the company's rewards and recognition systems are set up to provide positive incentives for increasing change capacity. You're able to see if recruiting efforts target people with the towering strengths needed for a change effort. In other words, you carry a great deal of credibility when you communicate that there is a major weakness relative to change capacity, and not just in the people area. When HR informs the boss that "we just don't have the talent to carry out the company's new strategy," that can be a provocative comment about strategic issues.

No matter what function you're in or leadership level you're at, you need to concern yourself with organizational assessment because of time and money issues. You may have just brilliantly assessed a group of people for their change capacity and created dynamite development plans, but you may be throwing away time and money if all your organizational pieces aren't in alignment. Specifically, you want to be able to answer the following question:

> Are our issues and problems too big for any kind of individual development effort to have much of an effect?

Let's say you need to develop thirty C-players into A-players within a year in order to achieve an organizational goal of becoming a global marketer. If you don't create versatile, change-responsive leaders with global marketing skills, the company will be at a serious competitive disadvantage. This is a tall development order with a pretty tight deadline. The issues and problems may well be too big for development to address. After an organizational assessment, you may want to recommend another course of action: recruiting or outsourcing to obtain the needed expertise and change leaders. Or your organizational assessment may convince you that the heart of the problem is an outmoded technological process or poor leadership.

The point is that you can determine if development is a realistic option or if other things need to happen in tandem with or before development for it to be effective. For instance, the only real solution to the organization's problems may be downsizing, reengineering, or some other form of restructuring. While you may not be in a position to recommend these options, you can at least make your position clear to your boss and explain why individual development alone isn't going to get the job done.

More commonly, your organizational assessment might reveal a flaw in strategy, processes, or implementation. You believe change capacity development will have a strong payoff if this flaw is addressed. You can therefore take or recommend actions that will complement the development of your people.

Let's examine the basic components of the change alignment model so that you'll understand what it is you need to assess organizationally.

Strategy

While there are many aspects to strategy, the two areas that you need to assess are strategic communication and leadership.

Communication

I know of a team leader who was responsible for formulating and implementing a plan to foster diversity even though the organization planned to divest itself of most of its foreign holdings (which had been the original impetus for increased diversity training). While the company still has a need for diversity training, the focus of that training had shifted. The team leader—who was not aware of the company's planned divestiture—was preparing his group for a change strategy that no longer existed.

This type of thing happens all the time, though the gap of understanding may be subtler than in this example. The larger the company, the greater the chance that strategy has been miscommunicated (or not communicated at all) or misinterpreted. Like the children's game "telephone," messages are passed from one person to the next and are slightly mangled as they're passed along. By the time the message moves through four or five layers, it bears little resemblance to the original communication.

It's not unusual for managers to complain that they are unclear about the organization's direction, and so they go off in a direction that they judge is appropriate. This can be problematic when managers are attempting to prepare their groups to meet a change challenge. While it's always a good idea to develop people so that they improve their change capacity, there needs to be some strategic guidance. If there isn't, the wrong A-player (e.g., someone lacking the necessary towering strength) can be put in a pivotal position or people won't be developed to meet a change strategy's deadline. In addition, crucial unanswered questions about people are ignored (e.g., "Will George be a good team player if he's placed in a cross-functional team?") because they seem to be of secondary importance. If managers understood a strategy correctly, they might realize that unanswered questions about employees will directly affect employees' ability to achieve a strategic objective. Senior managers typically are frustrated when a change strategy isn't being implemented effectively, and they often complain that middle managers "just don't get it" or they "don't want to change." In reality, the problem usually can be traced back to poor communication.

Specifically, senior management may communicate the words of what it wants but not the behaviors. It may give roughly the same speech about change strategy to managers that it gave to the investment community. While senior management may eloquently proclaim the need to be more innovative and take more decision-making risks, this doesn't help middle managers understand what new behaviors are desired and should be displayed. If, for instance, a sales manager is responsible for preparing her group to become more of a "partner" with customers and to conduct business in a less "transactional" manner (a result of a new partnering strategy drawn up by senior management), the sales manager can proceed in many different ways. Unless she is aware of what the partnering behaviors should be, she may develop people in ways that facilitate change, but not the type of change management wants. Or she might underestimate how significant the strategy is for the company and develop the change capacity of one individual when she should be developing four or five.

Senior management can distort the communication of strategy in many ways. For instance, some organizations give people too little information on the assumption that they know what the strategic expectations are. Others provide too much information so that people are hamstrung by all the data and directions they've received; they're immobilized by overly complex instructions and overbearing bosses who are intimidating everyone with their memos and directives.

As you assess and develop the change capacity of your people, take a little time to assess if the strategic goals have been communicated to you clearly. The following list of questions will help you make this assessment:

▲ Are you aware of the company's overall strategy and how it relates to your change capacity development plans?

▲ If there is a disconnect between what you understand the strategy to be and your particular, change-focused assignment, what is the cause? Have you received inaccurate information? Have you received insufficient information?

▲ Can you align your development activities with the overall strategy by seeking clarification from your boss? From your boss's boss? Will this information provide you with clear direction to assess the change capacity of your people and develop them to achieve strategic goals?

▲ Do you understand the time frame for implementing a change strategy? Given this time frame, can you develop the change capacity of your people so that they are ready to assume pivotal positions and provide support when you need them to be ready?

▲ If you are in the middle of the assessment/development process when you identify a disconnect, what is your most feasible option: to revamp your assessment/development approach, recruit the people you need, or outsource in order to bring in the appropriate talent?

Obviously, the best time to grasp the organizational change strategy is before you begin assessing for personal change capacity. Still, if you catch disconnects sufficiently early, you can often adjust your individual assessment and development tactics so that your people are prepared to carry out their piece of the strategy effectively.

Leadership

The other strategic element that must be assessed involves leadership. The heads of organizations as well as change leadership teams must be strongly and visibly committed and involved if change is going to roll out smoothly. While you cannot secure this commitment and involvement on your own, you need to know how much you can depend on leadership for resources and other forms of support. Even if you develop all your key people so that they reach their change capacity potential, you can still have trouble implementing a change strategy and achieving top results if you don't receive leadership support.

Here are some typical problems that result from lack of support:

▲ *A refusal to spend money on outside talent.* Your assessment may reveal that you simply have too many C-players and D-players and too little time to get your group up to change speed. If you don't bring in A-players and B-players or outsource some work, you can't achieve your part of the change strategy. Without strong leadership commitment, you'll be left in the lurch. It is important to know in advance whether you have to do everything internally. There is nothing worse than conducting an assessment under the false impression that you can go outside for talent if your assessment dictates that course of action. It's far better to know that you have to go it alone and plan accordingly than be surprised late in the game. If you are an HR person, you probably have a good reading on this issue; you know the politics of spending money on "stars" and what corporate policy is in this regard.

▲ *An unwillingness to give you the time you need.* Without leadership commitment, you may find resistance to your change capacity development plans. Specifically, you'll find that you are not allowed to develop people by allowing them to change jobs, learn from others, or restructure their jobs. All this "change capacity" time is time taken away from doing a job people are currently capable of doing. As a result, it may be viewed as unproductive work by the company's leadership if they don't value personal change capacity (and believe change is accomplished purely by dictate and direction rather than at the people level).

▲ *A fickle approach to change goals.* In other words, the change strategy communicated at the beginning of the process is altered or even negated before it really gets rolling. When leadership isn't committed to a change strategy, any bump in the road can cause the strategy to veer off course. A dip in revenue can cause leadership to become concerned about the change strategy's cost and table the effort for "a better time." A new opportunity, such as an exciting product introduction or an acquisition, can distract leadership from a larger change approach and cause them to lose interest. Or leadership may simply have second thoughts about a strategy because they've heard something negative about the change approach (e.g., an article in a trade magazine, a speaker at an association conference, a consultant who denigrates the strategy). In all these cases, your assessment criteria and development needs shift. You may find yourself developing the wrong people or basing your assessment on the wrong targeted skills. If you know that your leadership is fickle, you might want to assess and develop employees in as broad a way as possible. In other words, concentrate on improving the change capacity of a diverse group of people who will be prepared to achieve a variety of change goals (rather than just one, narrowly defined goal).

Fred Smith at Federal Express, Steve Ruzika at ADT Security Services, and Hugh McColl at Bank of America all are leaders who largely avoided these problems by demonstrating unusual commitment to and involvement with their organization's change efforts. Whenever Federal Express would introduce a new technology to its system, Smith was always a highly visible supporter of that technology and facilitated whatever was necessary to adapt to all the new processes and procedures. Ruzika talked constantly about people and customers, providing enthusiasm and energy for ADT to become a more customer-focused organization. McColl made sure everyone in the bank (and outside the company, for that matter) understood how committed he was to reshaping the organization.

Their opposite was a chairman of a large corporation that was attempting to reengineer itself in order to remain competitive. While the president of the company was a highly visible proponent of the changes that were occurring, the chairman distanced himself. As a result, many of the change efforts that were taking place throughout the company stalled. Many managers felt that the chairman's absenteeism signaled that they didn't have to become more versatile or change responsive. It became very difficult to convince people to develop new, needed skills or take on new roles and responsibilities. As a result, the reengineering effort failed and the organization has paid a high price for its adherence to the status quo.

It's not just the leader who counts. Assessing whether senior management is behind the change is crucial. If there is disagreement about a change strategy among the leadership coalition, it impacts how the strategy is executed. Sometimes it affects it because the disaffected leaders are open and even outspoken about their resistance to change. Morale plummets and the debate about a change strategy's validity spreads throughout the organization. But there are also times when senior managers publicly support the change but privately sabotage it (or if not sabotage, talk it down to peers and subordinates). They put the kibosh on change capability development plans or passively resist such plans by failing to provide resources or sponsorship.

Assessing leadership alignment can be done by answering the following questions:

▲ Is the CEO willing to put his reputation on the line by speaking out strongly and continuously in favor of the change strategy?

▲ Do you see evidence that the CEO is backing up his words with tangible support, such as creating change leadership teams, redirecting HR efforts to facilitate targeted changes, and making money available for change capacity development?

▲ If the change strategy fails, will the CEO be adversely affected; is the CEO aligned with the strategy to the point that he will be embarrassed if it fails and may even lose his job as a result?

▲ Do you find it difficult to obtain the time, cooperation of other people, sponsorship, and other resources necessary to develop your people to achieve increased change capacity?

▲ Are you or your employees confused by the messages sent by leadership about the change strategy?

▲ Does it seem as if senior management has different change agendas? Are there disagreements over the speed and cost of change as well as the specific programs that need to be transformed?

People

As I've made clear throughout this book, this is the most neglected area when it comes to change in organizations. While I'm not claiming it is the most important area, it is akin to the oil in a car. When I first received my driver's license, my father frequently told me, "Don't drive the car without checking the oil." What in the world is so important about oil, I wondered. Just try to drive a car without it and see what happens to the engine. While the engine may be more important than the oil in a relative sense, it's completely dependent on the oil and will break down without it. The change capability of people, like oil, is essential for a change mechanism to run smoothly and efficiently. The visionary CEO leader might drive change with strategy and communication skills, but if he's leading a bunch of C-players and D-players, the strategy isn't going to get far.

Rather than summarizing all the points covered earlier, I thought I'd give you a checklist that will help you assess whether people have been properly developed to lead and support change. Go through the following list and mark each point true or false for your organization:

True or False Checklist

☐ The majority of positions pivotal to planning and implementing a change strategy are staffed by A-players.

☐ Irreplaceable pros and other technically skilled individuals are given support positions suitable to their limited versatility (rather than rewarded with change leader positions).

☐ Change capacity assessments dictate whether you rely on development to meet the needs of a change strategy or turn to external sources of talent.

☐ D-players are moved out of the company or out of harm's way while C-players and B-players are encouraged to increase their change capacity and are given the time and development plans to do so.

☐ People with towering strengths are matched up with change positions that require targeted skills.

☐ An effort is made to develop change capacity bench strength.

☐ Unanswered questions don't hang over the heads of people placed in change leadership positions.

☐ The organization has change capacity profiles of most of its key people.

Processes

Whether you are being asked to change a manufacturing, design, customer service, hiring, or financial process or to make changes that in some way relate to an existing process, you need to assess the state of that process. A team of people with the highest possible change capacity will struggle in the face of a process that's deeply flawed.[3] A-players won't be able to create a successful new process if the new one has the same problems as the old one.

Processes can be highly technical, and you may lack the technical knowledge necessary to evaluate a process in depth. That's fine, since the point of this assessment isn't to pinpoint the process problem and solution but to give you a sense of what you are up against. You need to grasp the magnitude of your assignment so that you don't underestimate (or overestimate) your objective. If you need to design a new process to achieve your group's change objective, then you must recognize that fact in advance so that you can ask your boss for time and financial resources and HR for the support (i.e., recruiting) you require. This process assessment will also give you insight into the targeted skills that you need to match up with your people's towering strengths. You may discover that there's a specific process skill that is paramount to achieve an objective in your area, and it's one you don't currently possess.

There are two parts to this assessment:

1. Determining the current state of the relevant process
2. Figuring out how feasible it is for you to complete your assignment successfully, given the current state of the process

Assessment of the current process state can be done in a number of ways. You may have access to or have participated in a formal process assessment and therefore know exactly what the strengths and weaknesses in the process are. You can also conduct your own informal assessment by asking some simple questions and surveying your personal change capacity assessment team about these questions. I've found that the following types of questions work well for any process:

▲ What aspects of the existing process elicit the most frequent complaints; what are these complaints about?
▲ When people praise the process, what specific aspect do they praise?
▲ Has the process been subject to continuous improvement, sporadic improvement, or no improvement?
▲ Are there political or financial pressures that are keeping the process stuck in its current state?
▲ If you were to compare/contrast your process with the process of other organizations (e.g., where you or others formerly worked), how does it compare? Is it better, worse, or the same?
▲ Could the process be termed "state of the art"; if not, why?

Given the state of the process, how easy or difficult will it be for you to achieve your change goals? Perhaps a better way to look at this question is in terms of your group's requirements. Given the strengths and weaknesses of a process, determine whether your group needs the following resources to make change happen:

▲ *Time.* It will take *X* months to develop people to the point that they'll be capable of revamping the process.

▲ *Money.* It will require a significant investment in new equipment, software, or other tangible products for us to fulfill our change-focused assignment.

▲ *Skills.* We need people who have specific talents or knowledge (list them) to improve the process to a level acceptable for our group.

The other two possibilities are that you have no requirements or that you have impossible ones. In the former instance, you can achieve your change goals with the process exactly as it is. In the latter instance, the process is so far removed from where it should be that you believe your assignment is unfeasible.

You should articulate what your requirements are relative to a process sooner rather than later. I've worked with a number of organizations around customer process issues, and I've found that teams that identify their needs at the beginning of their work tend to produce much better results. One team was conducting a personal change capacity assessment with the ultimate aim of accelerating response time to customer information requests. First, however, the team had conducted an informal assessment of the customer service process and discovered that the high-tech Extranet the customer had insisted upon was creating service delays; the company's customer service people bitterly complained in private about the system but were afraid to do anything about it because the client had initiated it. Given this assessment, the team required someone with the towering strength of Extranet system design. This wasn't the only key to making change happen. The team also had to deal with the fact that too many customer service managers were well-placed and irreplaceable pros who lacked the versatility necessary to take on the added challenge of leading an effort to improve response time. However, the team was able to ensure it had the expertise necessary to make the right type of change.

Implementation

If you have the right strategy, people, and processes in place to drive change, then what can go wrong in the implementation phase? Many times, nothing goes wrong. If you have every-thing aligned, you have a strong chance of implementing a change strategy successfully. Still, I've seen instances where organizations have achieved this alignment yet implementation became a nightmare. Sometimes this happens for unfore-seen reasons that you can't assess in advance. A sudden dip in the economy or the company's revenues can rob a change strategy of the dollars and leadership attention it needs to be put in place effectively. An unexpected glitch in the technol-ogy upon which a new manufacturing process is based can throw everyone off.

What you can assess for, however, is measurement. How adept is your organization at measuring performance progress toward a goal? One of the hallmarks of any change strategy is that you are venturing into unexplored territory; there are no familiar signposts to mark the way. When groups attempt to make change happen within companies, they become disori-ented and dispirited unless they have a real sense that they are making progress. Even if they're not making progress, they need to locate themselves in relationship to their goal and have a sense of where they are falling short.

Some companies are strong believers in monitoring and measuring performance, and these companies tend to fare better during the implementation of change programs. Steve Ruzika, the president of ADT, believed so strongly in measure-ment that he would become personally involved in the cre-ation of measures. Once, he spent three days with security system installers, soliciting their input on how their perfor-mance should be measured. This is not typical of a CEO, but it demonstrated how he felt about people and the issue of mea-surement. They were formulating a new installation process, and he wanted to be sure that they were measured according to "real world" standards rather than ones dreamed up by an out-of-touch executive.

Concomitant with measures are rewards. Whereas some people are intrinsically motivated to lead and support change, others need extrinsic motivation. If your organization estab-lishes fair rewards (i.e., raises, promotions, incentives, and verbal approbation from bosses) linked to fair measures, it will give employees an incentive to embrace change during implementation. Putting in a new system and trying to get the kinks out can be frustrating. Attempting to move a group from a hierarchy to a team structure can be maddening. Encouragement in the form of tangible and intangible rewards can keep people moving forward to their goals.

Think about your company's performance regarding measures and rewards and assess it according to the following questions:

▲ Does your company set up fair and clear measures for performance?

▲ Are the measures realistic, or do they reflect an unrealistically optimistic viewpoint?

▲ Do most people have a good sense of "where they are" when they are working on projects? Do they receive regular feedback about their progress? Is there a more formal system in place that helps people see what their objectives are and how close (or how far) they are from achieving them?

▲ Are rewards usually linked to clear performance measures, or are they based on other factors (e.g., favoritism, seniority)?

▲ Are the rewards appropriate for the measures achieved, or do they seem inadequate?

Obviously, HR departments should have input into such things as measures and rewards for performance. They're the ones that often are involved in creating monitoring systems to measure people's development and ability to meet performance goals, and HR may well be responsible for leading the initiative in creating a system to measure change capacity improvements. While there are certainly other things to measure besides change capacity, this new measurement system needs to plug into measurements in other areas of the company. HR should take responsibility for making sure a linkage is made between change capacity improvements and positive results in areas such as turnover, system improvements, and even profitability. While this is a challenging task, it is also one that will be increasingly important if change capacity programs are going to survive and thrive.

Results

I want to emphasize that you shouldn't turn organizational assessment into a mammoth task. You can't be expected to do a full-blown, scientific assessment without enormous amounts of time and resources. Organizational assessment is, however, included in the change capacity process because it gives you a way to "eyeball" problems and issues outside of the people box that might become obstacles to your change efforts.

Alignment of strategy, people, processes, and change implementation simply means that everything is in place that change requires. What you are looking for in your organizational assessment are obvious deficits—a leader that is completely uninvolved in the change effort, a process that is from the dark ages. The good news is that organizations tend to be pretty good about keeping their strategy, processes, and implementation in alignment. Where organizations usually fail is in the people category, and your individual assessment and development work should have taken care of this problem, at least as far as your particular group is concerned.

Nonetheless, you don't want to have done all your people work only to let an organizational weakness trip you up. You need to consider the larger picture and determine if there is anything on the organizational level that might turn into trouble. If there is, the next chapter will suggest how you might deal with it.

I'd like to end this assessment chapter with a tool that several organizational leaders have used effectively to do a "quick read" of alignment issues. The Organization Alignment Audit is especially useful if you don't have the time to conduct a more detailed assessment or if you are a top executive who wants an overview of organizational issues before moving forward.[4]

Organization Alignment Audit

Purpose
This audit is a tool to assist leaders in assessing "present state" with factors that have proven to be key levers with change efforts within organizations.

Introduction
In considering organizational change, the major determinant of success is not necessarily the strategy; rather, implementation and alignment are the major "make or break" variables.

Key Factors in Driving Change
Strategy "Alignment . . . in the right direction"
▲ Strategic Focus
▲ Change Communications
▲ Senior Leadership Commitment

Key Capabilities "Focusing the Efforts"

▲ People:
  ☐ Talent Available
  ☐ Technical Core Competencies

▲ Process:
  ☐ Continuous Improvement of the Operations
  ☐ Customer Focus

Change Implementation Mechanisms "Sustaining Momentum"
▲ Key System Readiness
▲ Mission Control/Measurement

In evaluating whether the change/strategy can succeed, we have found that ten alignment areas and questions are useful to the senior management team in thinking through and implementing actions, or "taking the organization to the next level."

Instructions
On the following pages is a series of statements. Rate these statements as to how you see the organization *today*. At the end of each series you will be asked to provide the average score for that particular series. To obtain this number, add the total number of points and divide by the number of statements in that particular series.

Rating Scale

+3	Great Strength of Ours
+2	
+1	Some Strength
0	Neither Strength nor Weakness
−1	Some Weakness
−2	
−3	Significant Weakness of Ours

Using the rating scale provided, rate each of the following statements:

Strategy: Focus

#	STATEMENT	Score
1	Knowledge about the products/services offered and the customers/markets "we will have in 2–3 years" is understood.	
2	Our value proposition—what we provide that is unique and distinctive—is defined and well-understood.	

Average Score _____

Communications

#	STATEMENT	Score
3	Present—The business case for change (e.g., Why change? Why this strategy? Why now?) is understood/agreed to by the top team.	
4	Future—A compelling case of the future has been laid out that will motivate and stimulate action within the organization.	

Average Score _____

Senior Leader Commitment—the "Pathfinder"

#	STATEMENT	Score
5	Key individuals involved in the critical early stage of the change feel that the senior leader is personally involved and strongly committed to the strategy.	
6	Perception is clear in the ranks that the top leader is "out in front" on the change and demonstrates strong commitment.	

Average Score _____

Rating Scale

+ 3	Great Strength of Ours
+ 2	
+ 1	Some Strength
0	Neither Strength nor Weakness
− 1	Some Weakness
− 2	
− 3	Significant Weakness of Ours

Using the rating scale provided, rate each of the following statements:

Alignment of Leadership Team

#	STATEMENT	Score
7	A "guiding coalition of key leaders" for the future is in place—we have the team to make this strategy happen.	
8	The "guiding coalition of key leadership" takes a corporate perspective versus a vested interest to produce the results we need from the strategy.	

Average Score _____

People: Talent Available

#	STATEMENT	Score
9	Currently we have "A" talent in place and in the pipeline to successfully launch and be successful in the next fiscal year.	
10	We ask tough questions about people and are willing to make tough "people calls."	

Average Score _____

People: Technical Core Competencies

#	STATEMENT	Score
11	At the top, we know what core skills (i.e., "make or break" skills) are critical to our success over the next 12–18 months.	
12	We have the capacity to quickly acquire skills or retool those individuals necessary for our success—our training system is "fine-tuned."	

Average Score _____

Rating Scale
  + 3   Great Strength of Ours
  + 2
  + 1   Some Strength
    0   Neither Strength nor Weakness
  − 1   Some Weakness
  − 2
  − 3   Significant Weakness of Ours

Using the rating scale provided, rate each of the following statements:

Process: Continuous Improvement of Operations

#	STATEMENT	Score
13	Presently, the know-how and skills to improve our key processes are available.	
14	We have a strong commitment to improve our work processes—making them more "customer facing" or externally focused than internally efficient.	

Average Score   _____

Process: Customer Focus

#	STATEMENT	Score
15	"Customer mentality" (i.e., what the customer needs) determines and defines quality and value.	
16	Managing customer perceptions of quality and value is as important as what is actually delivered.	

Average Score   _____

Change Implementation: Key System Readiness

#	STATEMENT	Score
17	Our people have support systems (e.g., selection, training, compensation) necessary to drive the change.	
18	Our overall performance system is geared to drive the strategy.	

Average Score   _____

Rating Scale

+3	Great Strength of Ours
+2	
+1	Some Strength
0	Neither Strength nor Weakness
−1	Some Weakness
−2	
−3	Significant Weakness of Ours

Using the rating scale provided, rate each of the following statements:

Change Implementation: Mission Control/Measurement

#	STATEMENT	Score
19	We keep score, track, and celebrate the progress we're making.	
20	Oversight and follow-through ensure that we stay on the right path and pursue it to our destination.	

Average Score   _____

Scoring

Please score your survey, using the summary scale provided on the following page.

Present Status of Alignment Factors

1. Strategic Focus	2. Change Communications	3. Senior Leadership Commitment	4. Alignment of Leaders	5. Talent Available	6. Core Competencies	7. Continuous Improvement of Operations	8. Customer Focus	9. Key System Readiness	10. Mission Control/ Measurement	
										+3 Significant Strength
										+2
										+1 Some Strength
										Neutral
										−1 Some Weakness
										−2
										−3 Significant Weakness

INSTRUCTIONS: Transfer your Average Scores to this sheet; connect the dots to see the pattern.

12

How Leaders at All Levels Can Make Change Happen

Based on your organizational assessment, you should have a sense of how ready your organization is to support your efforts to spearhead change. Some organizations will be more ready than others. Your company may have been moribund for years and it is only going to be change-ready when all the elements discussed in Chapter 11—strategy, people, process, and change implementation—are revamped. This takes time, resources, and a leader willing to take on this enormous challenge.

This chapter will focus on what *you* can do to facilitate change in your particular area. The first and easiest thing you can do that will have the greatest impact is work with those in your organization who can provide you with the opportunity to recruit and develop A-players as well as the power to remove C-players and D-players from pivotal positions. (These issues will be covered in a bit more detail later in this chapter.) Every manager can also take a number of actions to affect strategy, process, and change implementation in ways that increase the odds that she will carry out her change assignments successfully.

First, let's talk about a "wild card" factor that usually plays a significant role in whether change is carried out effectively.

No Pain, No Gain

The more an organization is hurting, the more willing it is to try something new and different. While there are exceptions to this rule, the typical company usually doesn't start transforming its strategy, culture, and structure until the status quo is dysfunctional. In the late 1980s, Xerox Corp. embarked on a transformation process because its profitability was plummeting and the situation had reached crisis proportions. At ADT Security Services, changes only occurred when customers clearly communicated that they lacked confidence in the company's service. The pain was real and undeniable, and this fact made people more responsive to change strategies. Again, the skill of Steve Ruzika surfaced the pain, and we, as a senior management team, were able to act on this discrepancy.

Again, the keyword is *people.* The personal change capacity we've been talking about throughout this book is often directly proportional to the amount of pain an individual is experiencing. In other words, if someone in an organization truly believes he will be out of a job in three months unless his group makes significant changes, his change responsiveness and versatility scores can improve significantly (though once the crisis passes and he feels secure, his responsiveness and versatility will probably decline; thus, the need for meaningful change capacity development). Most of the time, however, people aren't in such catastrophic situations. More commonly, the pain is significant but managers shield them from the hurt. I've seen manager after manager fail to inform employees about the seriousness of a competitor's innovation, the impact of a quality problem, or the degree of dissatisfaction among customers. This failure is usually a result of a manager's desire not to cause panic and prevent lowered morale and turnover.

While you certainly don't want to panic people, you do want them to understand how serious the situation is and the potential negative consequences. Therefore, communicate the pain. At the same time, counterbalance the pain with a vision of what might be. If you can help employees see how both they and the company will be better off if they take on new roles and responsibilities, become more receptive to new ideas and processes, and implement a specific change strategy success-fully, then you provide a clear incentive for them to participate with enthusiasm and energy.

In fact, I think it would be great for organizations if their human resources (HR) departments built "pain communica-tion" modules into their training for young and new managers. As part of this effort, HR could let emerging leaders know that in this particular organization, problems aren't hidden but ex-plained and discussed. Such training might also provide man-agers with tools and techniques for delivering bad news in productive, motivating ways.

Up the Middle: A Shorthand Method to Determine How You Can Have the Greatest Impact

If you don't have the time to do a thorough and detailed orga-nizational assessment—and I'm assuming that many of you are being pushed hard to make change happen—then you can take a shortcut. Three factors most influence whether change is successful:

1. Having strong, supportive change leadership at the top (i.e., strategy)
2. Having the ability to obtain or develop A-players (i.e., people)
3. Having processes that are externally focused (i.e., process)

While the first two factors are self-explanatory, the last one needs a bit of explanation. Internally focused processes are those that are the equivalent of a self-absorbed person. An in-ternally focused manufacturing process, for instance, is 100 percent centered on technical matters. Manufacturing people give no thought to customer expectations or manufacturing technologies of competitors. Similarly, an internally focused sales process revolves around meeting sales quotas; there is scant consideration of helping customers grow and develop their businesses through products and services or attention to larger economic or social trends that might affect sales and service. A process that incorporates an external focus is much more responsive to change because it is sensitive to the many factors mandating change. Internally centered processes resist change because they are operating in their own world; they don't allow outside ideas and needs to shape the process.

In baseball, there's a phrase, "strong up the middle," which means a team is solid at catcher, pitcher, second base, shortstop, and center field. The belief is that these are the key positions for a baseball team, the ones that ultimately determine its success. I've just described the up-the-middle factors for change management success.

Look over your organizational assessment and determine which areas are solid. Based on your assessment, use the following guide to determine how you can positively impact change:

▲ *Solid in none of the areas.* If this is the case, you are fighting an uphill battle, and that's putting it optimistically. Without processes that promote change or leadership that supports it, you may end up developing personal change capacity in a vacuum. Without A-players or the time or resources to develop them, you probably will struggle to make change happen with B-, C-, and D-players. There isn't much you can do organizationally besides developing the change capacity of your people as best you can.

▲ *Solid in one of the areas.* This is a hopeful sign. You can use your strength in one area as leverage for the others. In other words, if you have plenty of A-players, you can communicate this fact to senior management. You can also add this qualifier: They are ready, willing, and able to drive change, only they can't do it without additional support. With strong leadership support, you can leverage an increased external focus in a targeted process. Which of the two areas should be selected as the one to develop? In most instances, the less-

weak area is the best candidate (because it may need strength-
ening but not development from scratch).

▲ *Solid in two or three areas.* If you are strong in all three
areas, you can simply cherry-pick problems; it may be that
your only development need is to get HR more active in recruiting talent. If you're strong in two areas, then your obvious
task is to do what you can to develop the third. This is relatively easy, since now you have two strong areas to leverage to
achieve change agendas.

What you can do to make an organizational contribution
to change depends on your position and change mandate. Let's
begin with the three most common actions managers can take
to facilitate change.

Having Supportive Leaders at the Top

While you can't replace uncommitted, change-averse leaders
with A-players, you can lobby the leaders you are in contact
with—your boss and your boss's boss—for more time, resources, and budgets to make change happen. In many cases,
there's a significant amount of latent support for change
among management and especially among top HR executives
who are struggling with impossible requests for more change
agents. It's latent because of a wide variety of factors—politics,
a long-standing culture of hope and accommodation, risk-
aversion in a down year, among other factors. If you put forth
your change proposition forcefully and convincingly, you may
sway an organizational leader to lend you a hand.

In one large pharmaceutical company, Lois, the sales and
marketing manager, was attempting to shift away from trade
advertising in medical publications and toward direct-to-
consumer television advertising. This involved not only a
budgetary shift but recruiting people with direct-to-consumer
expertise and developing that expertise internally. Perhaps
more significantly, it also meant that people in the department
had to learn to value a direct-to-consumer marketing approach

and be less dependent on the old customer relationships with doctors and medical facilities.

While Lois had received her boss's approval for this change initiative, it was given reluctantly. "Isn't there any way we can avoid such a radical step?" he had asked. There wasn't; a competitor was running direct-to-consumer print ads that were the talk of the industry, and it was important for the company to create its own approach quickly. Unfortunately, Lois found that it was difficult to move as quickly as she needed to. For one thing, she was not allowed to take maximum advantage of the HR training and development group. Lois was told by the head of HR that they didn't have time or resources to spare in helping her achieve her change strategy objectives. "There are higher priorities," the HR director bluntly told her (obviously, this HR head was not one of those who ardently supports change). For another, her employees weren't convinced that her strategy was aligned with the corporate strategy; they kept hearing the CEO and other senior managers talk about how the company was in great shape and that it would not be subject to the downsizing, reengineering, and other transformations besetting other organizations.

Finally, Lois realized that she needed to secure management support if she was going to transition her department effectively. She met with her boss and presented him with a carefully prepared scenario of what would happen if the company failed to shift to a direct-to-consumer focus, a scenario that emphasized negative financial implications. Her work, combined with her willingness to take a risk by endorsing this change strategy, convinced him to lobby in her behalf. Using his considerable influence and political savvy, he managed to get his boss—a senior vice president—on board, and soon Lois had the HR support she required. In addition, most of the company's senior leaders also refrained from further "everything's fine, don't worry" statements.

If your assessment reveals a lack of leadership commitment to whatever change you are attempting to implement (and unlike Lois, it may be a change mandated from above that's receiving only token support), try the following methods to push the organization in the right direction:

▲ *Create a convincing, formal presentation demonstrating where leadership commitment is needed.* This doesn't simply mean talking to your boss about the problem; you need to present it formally to your boss. As Lois did, take the time to create a written document that makes a case for leadership support. Using facts and figures as well as projections of positive and negative scenarios; put together a written argument that demonstrates what specific leadership commitment you require and how it will benefit the company. In addition, make sure that you don't present your case as a complaint or with a whining tone. Emphasize the positive consequences of leadership-supported change as well as the negative consequences if such support is lacking.

▲ *Gather support on your level first.* Many times, other managers at your level are in the same position as you are. This is especially true if you are all being asked to implement a piece of the same change strategy; your team, department, division, or plant is required to make change happen as part of a larger plan. It is likely that if you're lacking time, money, or other resources, so too is your counterpart in another function or office. You probably can also garner support from HR professionals. If, for instance, you are all lacking the A-players necessary to drive change, then you can present a united front and ask management for training or recruiting help. Strength in numbers is important when asking for leaders to make a greater commitment to change.

▲ *Target the most change-empathetic leader.* This might not be your boss or even your boss's boss. At least one senior manager, however, is likely to recognize how crucial change is and take up your cause. Sometimes this person is easily identified; she's the one who has consistently and vocally demonstrated a commitment to significant organizational change. Other times this person is operating covertly, especially in cultures of hope and accommodation. You may have to ferret this leader out by talking to your boss or other managers on your level about who might have the clout and the willingness to garner support for organizational change. Ideally, this will be someone who believes that change happens one person at a time and is committed to a change capacity assessment and development process. Once you find this individual, you need to present your problem and solution in the same formal way that you would present it to your boss.

Having the Ability to Obtain or Develop A-Players

If you're not blessed with A-players, you need to find some way to get them in your group. Put simply, change won't happen without A-players. You can have as many highly skilled C-players or even change-facilitating B-players as you want, but if you don't have individuals who embrace and lead change and take on new roles and responsibilities, you're going to come up short.

Fortunately, there's a great deal you can do in this area on your own. Without organizational support, you can still develop the change capacity of your people to a certain extent. With support, however, it's a much easier process and one much more likely to yield A-players.

It's easier to make change happen in organizations with strong HR functions that understand how to build personal change capacity. These companies have HR people who are highly responsive to development and recruiting needs of various managers. They can provide various job restructuring and reassignment opportunities so that employees can increase their change responsiveness and versatility. They can also help individuals develop towering strengths that line up with targeted skills. In short, HR is tuned into the personal change capacity process and has the authority to work with you to maximize that process.

What happens, however, if your HR function is in sorry shape? Then it makes your job that much tougher. You can't transform the HR group overnight, even if you are a top executive or even if you are an HR professional yourself. But what you can do is work toward establishing a good relationship with key HR professionals. I've found that most HR functions are filled with good people who are hamstrung by a lack of knowledge about personal change capacity or by a management mind-set that limits the HR department's role to recruitment, selection, training, benefits, and compensation but does not encourage HR to venture into change capacity territory. As I've emphasized throughout this book, however, HR professionals can be valuable allies in the quest for improved change capacity.

You can develop organizational change capacity in a small but significant way if you make it your business to educate HR professionals about how much they can contribute to a company's change strategy. Admittedly, this isn't a one-meeting assignment. It means cultivating relationships with HR people and working closely with them so they understand how they can facilitate your group's change goals. I've seen managers in many organizations who have recognized the critical role HR can play and extracted tremendous resources from HR in their change efforts. I know one functional manager who worked with his HR person to search the company for A-players and B-players; the HR director helped assess a number of candidates and helped some of them join the functional manager's change team. HR people are potential change capacity heroes, and if you are working in an HR function you should take the chance to be a hero; the odds are it will help both your career and your company.

This brings up another important point: Organizational change capacity is contingent on a system that encourages placing the right people in the right positions and removing the wrong ones. If seniority still has a strong place in your culture, then it is going to be difficult for you to remove C-players and D-players from pivotal positions. As problematic as this situation is, you can still manipulate the system if you establish good relationships with HR people and if you work with your boss on the problem. What will help you are your individual and group change capacity assessments. You can go to HR or your boss and say, "Mike, who is in a pivotal position in our group, is a D-player, which means we can be sure he's going to do everything possible to resist this change strategy." Communicating the change capacity methodology and using the shorthand of A-, B-, C-, and D-players goes a long way toward enlisting the support of higher-ups and your peers for what you're trying to achieve. I've learned that other managers resonate strongly to change capacity ideas once they grasp them; they recognize how important it is to place A-players in pivotal positions and remove D-players.

The other key issue is convincing management that you need to recruit A-players if you lack them internally or don't have the time to develop them. Again, your change capacity assessment results will help make a case for recruiting. Ideally, you'll be able to enlist the support of your boss as well as other executives for a corporatewide policy using change capacity assessments as a recruiting guide. Realistically, this may be a tough argument to make because recruiting A-players can become expensive. A more practical goal may be to secure agreement and a budget to bring in at least one A-player from the outside if the internal situation looks bleak and your change assignment requires immediate action.

Having Processes That Are Externally Focused

In your assessment of processes, you may have discovered a wide variety of problems, from lack of state-of-the-art technology to new processes that no one knows how to use effectively. Many of these problems are relatively simple to identify and solve. If a process isn't moving fast enough and everyone is complaining about it, the people responsible have to try and fix it. If they won't or can't fix it—if management is in deep denial or if the fix costs too much—there's not much you can do. Procentries, under the leadership of Eric Berliner is the benchmark provider. They have tied all of their work to financial outcomes.

A much more insidious and common problem, however, relates to processes that ignore the outside world, especially the customer. I'm not just referring to the sales or customer service process but all the processes, both big and small, within an organization. What happens is that the manufacturing process becomes enmeshed in the nitty-gritty details of making a product or the information technology (IT) process becomes wrapped up in software esoterica. In other words, the process becomes the focus of the process rather than larger business objectives.

When this happens, change is a bear. Internally focused processes are inflexible, resisting new ideas and approaches from the outside. While the process owners may be receptive to a new internal idea—IT people are quite willing to test and use an exciting new piece of software—they are close-minded regarding anything not strictly related to the process itself. The finance process, for instance, will resist changes to accounts receivable methods that would meet customers' needs better. This resistance isn't to meeting customer needs as much as it is to reshaping the process itself.

If this is a problem for your organization, you need to address the particular process that is most important to your change effort by:

1. *Discussing the situation with the person who is in charge of the process.* Sometimes process heads will respond positively if you communicate how crucial their process is to a change strategy. They may be willing to accommodate the needs of such a strategy because leadership is pushing hard for its change agenda. If so, explain the particular customer concerns you have and volunteer to work with this individual to improve the process.

2. *Appealing to an organizational change leader.* Realistically, you're going to find some process owners unwilling to listen to your suggestions; you may lack sufficient influence within the organization or they may be C-players and D-players unwilling to make their processes more externally focused. In these instances, you have to do an end-run around them and appeal to an organizational change leader. These change agents may be willing to run interference for you. In fact, it is often part of the mandate handed to them by the CEO. A good change leader will be astute about how a process is inhibiting change and will be skilled at reconnecting it to customer requirements.

3. *Giving voice to your own customer champions.* The process at issue may be one that you control or are in some

way responsible for. If you can't single-handedly externalize the process, you certainly can move it in that direction. One way of doing so is making sure the customer champions in your group are involved on process assessment and restructuring teams. Customer champions are easy to identify. They're frequently raising customer issues; they're the ones who bring up customer questions and complaints and who directly or indirectly listen to what customers have to say. At the very least, pay attention to these champions. They have the knowledge and ability to open up processes in ways that will facilitate whatever change strategy you are trying to implement.

Developing Across-the-Board Change Capabilities

Developing organizational strengths in up-the-middle areas is your first and best step, but it isn't your only one. Your assessment may have turned up other deficiencies related to strategy, people, process, and implementation. After you've addressed up-the-middle concerns, you'll also want to consider the following possibilities.

Strategy Solution: Change Communications

The most common problem is that a change strategy has not been communicated clearly, and a disconnect exists between your work on a change strategy and the overall corporate objective.[1] Sometimes the disconnect is minor, but in other instances the disconnect involves time frame, methods, and goals. If the problem is a onetime event (e.g., miscommunication about a deadline), then it usually can be resolved by talking with your boss. Unfortunately, problems like this tend to be ongoing; one miscommunication begets another. A pattern unfolds in which there is continuous uncertainty about what, when, and how something should be done. Because of secrecy surrounding a change strategy, layers of management between "thinkers" and "doers," and the complexity of some change strategies, miscommunication is a recurring theme.

If the source of this miscommunication has to do with technical access to information, work with your IT group so that it can plug you into what you need to know when you need to know it. This often isn't a big deal. Intranet systems can greatly facilitate information exchanges and make sure your change efforts remain aligned with corporate strategy.

More serious communication problems involve secrecy, bureaucracy, and complexity. It may be that your and even your boss's pleas for better information about the change agenda aren't heeded. You may have to present a convincing case to management about the need for a faster, clearer information flow relative to change. One of the best ways to present such a case is to benchmark another organization (or more than one) that has learned how to communicate change strategy properly. Benchmarking, if done properly, provides irrefutable evidence that superior strategic communication results in better implementation of change. While you or subordinates may be able to do this benchmarking, it's more likely that you'll need to call in a consultant.

Implementation Solution: Measures

Because change can be so complex and confusing to implement, it's helpful to provide your people with a set of signposts. Ideally, your organization will have such a system in place that you can take advantage of, a system that your assessment revealed as fair and useful. If they don't, you should create a simple but effective action plan yourself, starting by asking and answering the following three questions:

▲ What has to be done?
▲ Who should do it?
▲ When will it be done? And by whom?

Change is especially scary when it actually starts to happen. Then it's easy for B-players and C-players to lapse into old habits even if they've been coached and developed out of traditional patterns of behavior. They may be more responsive to change and more versatile in certain situations, but when they're actually asked to implement a major new program or to transform a work environment, they may retreat to old attitudes and behaviors. This is less likely to happen with good measures in place. Even though people are doing new and different things, when they can ground themselves in measures, they have a sense of what they've accomplished and what they still have to do.

People Solution: Outsourcing

This one is simple. If your assessment determines that you lack the A-players and you don't have the time or money to develop or recruit them, outsourcing may be a practical option. This doesn't mean terminating everyone in your group and giving all the work to an outside company. But it can mean finding a group of outside A-players who can handle certain responsibilities that your team cannot. I know of one team in a midsize company where no one possessed an essential towering strength in foreign acquisitions, yet this team was being asked to target good acquisition candidates in Pacific Rim countries. It brought in a consultant who supplemented the skills the team lacked.

The action here is to become familiar with outside sources who might be able to help you achieve your change goals. This means developing a list of sources, requesting written information, and taking the time to meet with some of these sources. Too many managers desperately struggling to find help with a change strategy are woefully unfamiliar with outside sources. As a result, they either choose to go it alone or select the wrong company to help them. Though this step will be time-consuming, it's time well spent, given the importance of people in making change happen.

Building Change Leadership Skills in Yourself and Your Direct Reports

It's very difficult for organizations with closed-off, dictatorial, and manipulative leaders to build change capacity. To increase change responsiveness and versatility, people need to take risks; they need to be encouraged to try new things; and they need to talk with someone who will empathize with their challenges. Your organizational assessment may not have revealed whether your organization's leadership is deficient in this regard; it's a difficult thing to assess through a formal analysis. But you probably have a good sense of what type of leader you and your direct reports are. You can greatly facilitate your group's ability to achieve change objectives by adopting certain leadership practices.

First, be an influential leader rather than a powerful one. This distinction has received a significant amount of attention, but not in relation to change capacity. An organization of influencers can encourage, motivate, and energize people about building their change capacity. Influence makes people reflect upon issues and gives them an opportunity to think long and hard about their behaviors in changing situations. Power makes people respond without much thought; it invites a surface reaction that doesn't have much impact on change responsiveness or versatility. The more influential managers you have, the easier it will be to move a change agenda forward.

Second, create excitement, activity, and momentum around change projects. Some organizations treat change strategies as if they were dry, by-the-numbers programs. Or worse, they convey the notion that "this is something we have to do." Rather than making change strategies seem like drudgery, leaders need to super-energize people around change. This can mean everything from celebrations when change signposts are reached to talks in which the vision of an evolving future is shared. It can also mean creating a sense of "competitive urgency," demonstrating that the changes being made are related to the competitive environment and how everyone is engaged in a race to change fast and first.

Third, reward successful change projects. Don't be the type of leader who preaches how important change is but fails to practice this belief. Provide soft and hard rewards, especially for individuals and groups who have improved their change capacity and met change goals. It may be that your company's compensation system is tied to traditional performance reviews that don't take change capacity into account. As much as you and your direct reports can, factor in change capacity to bonuses and raises. You should make sure that A-players are not only financially rewarded but receive verbal accolades, freedom to work as they choose, and other perks at your disposal.

Change leadership starts at the top, and it's unfortunate if you happen to be saddled with someone at the top who is a D-player. But even if this worse-case scenario applies to you, you can still practice strong change leadership in your corner of the company.

Assessing Yourself

Finally, you can make a tremendous contribution to the organization's change capacity by assessing yourself. If every HR executive and managerial leader did this, the change capacity of a company would rise exponentially. In fact, one of the questions I hear from executives who are assessing others is: "How do I figure out my own change capacity?" It's likely that you have a good change capacity rating if you are taking the time to do the assessment and development this approach ro quires. It doesn't mean, however, that you don't have room for improvement. It's also possible that you might believe it's important for others to develop their change capacity as long as you don't have to do anything different.

As a leader, it's important to set the right example. I've known CEOs who expected their people to make significant changes in their work habits and to implement radical new strategies, but they themselves refused to take on more or different responsibilities. Sometimes this isn't as much a conscious refusal to become more versatile as it is focusing on everyone else to the exclusion of oneself.

Ideally, your boss and her team will have conducted a change capacity assessment of you and created a development plan based on that assessment. It's possible, however, that your boss is unwilling to do so. If this is the case, you have two options. First, you can ask someone you trust and respect in HR or elsewhere in the organization to conduct the assessment along the lines described in this book. While they may not be able to assemble a team to assess your change capacity, they probably can give you a good sense of your change responsiveness, versatility, towering strengths, and challenges/ unanswered questions.

If you feel uncomfortable asking someone to provide this assessment (or if you don't feel they understand the change capacity concepts well enough to do a good job), then you can conduct a self-assessment. While it is no substitute for an objective assessment by a qualified team, answering the following questions will give you a rough guesstimate of your capacity:

1. Think about the most recent instance in which your boss or organization instituted a new strategy, program, or plan and it directly affected your work life. Did you respond positively, negatively, or indifferently?

2. Write down the three most significant changes in your work life over the past ten years (e.g., a new job, a new boss, your company was acquired, your job was phased out and you had to learn a new one). Which of the following words best characterizes your overall reaction to these changes: excitement, cautious optimism, acceptance, skepticism, or hostility?

3. If you were asked to take on more responsibilities or additional roles in your current position, would you be excited about the chance to do more or angry that you were being asked to do more?

4. If you were asked to take on unfamiliar or difficult tasks that required you to acquire new skills and knowledge, would you be excited about this opportunity or resent that your new assignment required you to "stretch"?

5. Is there a work skill or task that you are particularly good at? If so, does it match up with what is increasingly needed by your group or the organization?

6. Do you feel concerned or uncertain about your ability to perform well in certain situations? It is possible that you might leave the company at some time in the near future?

7. Do you believe you have the type of personality that responds well in most changing situations, but has an Achilles' heel when asked to lead or participate in certain types of change?

As you can tell, the first two questions focus on change responsiveness, the next two on versatility, the fifth on towering strengths, the sixth on challenge/unanswered questions, and the seventh on change idiosyncrasies. Admittedly, this self-assessment is rudimentary and subject to your own misreading of who you are and how you deal with change. At the same time, if you are honest and perceptive about yourself, it will give you a way to calculate if you're a good leader or supporter of change strategies.

Epilogue: Change Begins One Person at a Time . . . But It Adds Up

Whether you are a human resources (HR) staff member, a line manager, or a top executive, you have a role to play in increasing the change capacity of your organization. In flattened organizations where decision making is delegated downward, all types of managers can play an important role in driving change in their teams, departments, plants, and business units. As the role of the HR department continues to be redefined—as they become less the minders of policies and procedures and more the developers of talent—there are more opportunities than ever before to help employees increase their change responsiveness and versatility.

In most companies, there are pockets of change capability activity, and even these pockets produce impressive results. Even more impressive, however, is when a significant number of managers within a company are all assessing and developing personal change capacity. At ADT, the cumulative change capacity assessments helped transform a stodgy, bureaucratic company, resulting in an influx of A-players and a departure of C-players and D-players from the top three management levels. While there were many indicators that this change strategy was a success, one of the most obvious ones was that the stock price doubled after the strategy was implemented.

At NationsBank, this change capacity approach was used

in various teams and groups to place people in pivotal positions who possessed the towering strengths those positions required and who could take on the increasingly varied responsibilities the changing nature of the business demanded. Again, the organization profited from these efforts, becoming sufficiently versatile that it could adapt successfully to a fast-moving financial environment.

In this final chapter, I'd like to leave you with some guidelines and troubleshooting tips that will facilitate implementing this approach in your organization. I've found that my clients tend to ask roughly the same questions about what they can do to maximize the impact of a change capacity program, and I suspect they're the same questions that have occurred to you. Therefore, let's begin with the most obvious one: How do I get started?

Launching Your Own Change Capacity Program

Ideally, you are part of an organization where personal change capacity assessments are mandated by top management and there are many other groups charged with assessing and developing their people's capacity. Realistically, you may be doing this program on your own, recognizing that it is the best way to help your group reach its objectives.

If the latter is the case, then the following advice may prove useful:

▲ *Keep the focus on the customer.* Make a case that your change capability assessment and development efforts will benefit the company's customers. Your boss is more likely to support your efforts if you can link improved change responsiveness and versatility to better customer service or improved product quality. I've found that this is almost always the case, but you may have to do some homework—talking to customers, doing more formal research, and involving sales functions. Too often, change is viewed as a purely internal affair, and this limited view detracts from its importance. Demonstrating how change confers external benefits (i.e., on customers) elevates its importance.

▲ *Recruit an action-oriented HR person.* This has been a recurring theme throughout this book for a reason: HR is the guardian of every organization's human asset inventory. HR departments know more about the people in your company and the tools for maximizing their value than anyone else. Enlist their help early and you'll benefit later; they can help you link your assessment and development efforts to the company's HR. And if you are an HR professional, you should be proactive and reverse-recruit a manager who needs to increase the change capacity of the group.[1]

▲ *Test-market change capacity principles internally.* Sometimes it takes a "demonstration" before management buys in to your change efforts. In other words, you need to show it this change capacity stuff works. This might mean replacing an assessed D-player with an A-player, or it could involve a development plan designed to increase the change capacity of someone occupying a pivotal position. Showing often has a more galvanizing effect than telling. The key, however, is your willingness to take the risk and move out C-players who are irreplaceable pros but who will ultimately fail to push your change agenda forward. Or the risk might simply be to bring in someone who lacks the proper seniority or traditional skill sets in favor of someone who is an active change responder. Communicate what you've done to your boss or other appropriate executives and see if they get it.

Giving A-Players More Than a Place to Work: The Need for Opportunities, Incentives, and Support

Some organizations mistakenly believe that if they can stockpile a sufficient number of A-players, they'll possess the change capacity necessary to implement even the most ambitious strategy. While it is true that A-players who are active responders and highly versatile are the best people to lead change efforts, there's no guarantee that they *will* lead those efforts or lead them well. There's also no guarantee that you can recruit all the A-players you need. While it would be great if you had an unlimited budget for recruiting these stars, A-players are expensive. People who have successfully driven change at other organizations know their worth, and they don't come cheap.

Maximizing the value of the A-players you have or the potential A-players you might develop are the real keys. Here are some suggestions about what you might do:

▲ *Make sure your A-players are pivotally placed.* You need to be willing and able to move A-players into pivotal change positions. This can be a problem for many reasons. Most often, managers are reluctant to displace a senior person who occupies that position, even if he's a C-player or D-player. If they have an A-player in their group, they hope she can contribute from a nonleadership position. More likely, the A-player will not only fail to contribute but become frustrated and leave. You need to manage with your head and not your heart.

▲ *Determine whether your A-players are really A-players.* Organizations that substitute performance appraisals or psychological tests for change capacity assessments frequently make this mistake. Because employees perform well or seem to have a change-positive personality, organizations automatically assume that they are A-players. In reality, they lack the versatility or change responsiveness that change leadership demands. Even if you use the tools in this book, however, you can make mistakes in assessment based on biases or false optimism. I've seen teams dub someone an A-player because they desperately need one and this individual was the best of the bunch assessed. I've also seen individuals referred to as A-players because they are the best we have. It is not who is here, but how they stack up to the definitions provided for change response and versatility—those are the calibration points. I've also seen teams rationalize their A-player choices, saying, "He'll grow into the role." You need to be brutally honest and objective in your assessment.

▲ *Compensate A-players accordingly.* If you don't fight for increased compensation for your most change-ready people, you are likely to discourage and even lose them. A dispirited A-player may perform like a B-player. The individual who feels underpaid and underappreciated may leave for a company that desperately needs change leadership.[2]

▲ *Refocus development on A-players rather than "problem children."* Some companies focus development on their C-players and D-players, assuming that A-players and B-players are doing just fine and don't need much help. They use development as a rehabilitation tool, hoping against hope that they can salvage their investment in an employee. When it comes to change capacity, however, a development dollar invested in an A-player has a much greater return than one invested in a D-player. Just because someone is an A-player doesn't mean she can't improve in some area. Even active responders and clearly versatile people can reach a higher level; they can learn to take on a wider variety of roles, respond with even greater energy and innovation to change, and acquire targeted skills that will make a specific change strategy more effective. There is no ceiling on change capacity; there is always room to become more versatile and change responsive.

If you need any more incentive to maximize the effectiveness of your A-players, you should be aware of a longitudinal PIMS study conducted at Harvard that revealed A-players produced 37 percent profit growth, B-players created 4 percent profit growth, C-players maintained the status quo, and D-players incurred a 7 percent profit loss.[3] At ADT we utilized these results when we reworked the talent pool. While the study defined these players in somewhat different terms than those used for change capacity, the point is equally relevant: A-players can have a tremendous impact on the bottom line if they're used properly.

A Small Cadre of A-Players Can Create a Grade-A Organization

Perhaps the best lesson I can leave you with is that change just isn't that hard to make happen if you have the right talent in the right places. It doesn't require a company to recruit 500 A-players instantly, nor does it demand an army of consultants, a strategy worthy of a battlefield general, or a CEO to put the fear of the status quo into employees.

In most organizations, there are relatively few pivotal people needed to drive a given change strategy. Change capacity assessments don't have to be conducted for every employee or every manager. If a change is targeted and requires only a few different teams to work on a project, just assessing and developing a few people for pivotal positions might do the trick.

The objective for most companies, however, is not simply to implement a short-term change strategy but build change muscle for the long term.[4] In other words, if you can identify the forty pivotal positions that will lead change in your organization for the next five years, then your ultimate goal is to fill each of these positions with an A-player. If you have teams throughout the company doing the type of assessment and development I've suggested here, it is entirely possible that you can achieve this goal in a matter of months.

One of the attributes of this process is that it takes advantage of available knowledge. No one has to conduct complex psychological testing or spend weeks interpreting the results of these tests. Everything boils down to people who know a given individual identifying her past responses to change and making educated guesses about her versatility in a changing future. Organizations fail to realize how much they know about their people's ability to support and lead change. All they require is a process for assessing and developing this capacity.

Change isn't going to go away. Continuous transformation will be a challenge for every company in the foreseeable future. This challenge cannot be met by strategic planning, visionary leadership, restructuring, and technology investments alone. As important as these and other factors are, they require the right people in the right positions if change is going to have a chance of succeeding. Minimally versatile, blocked change responders who are in pivotal positions will render the most brilliant strategy ordinary and find a way to subvert even the largest investment in new processes and equipment. Now and especially in the future, the competitive edge will go to organizations that support change capacity assessment and development. They will be the ones that will adapt faster and better to their evolving environments.

Is your organization change-capable? Ask the following five questions of your company and see how it fares:

1. Have the majority of managers in pivotal positions been assessed along change capacity lines?

2. Have the majority of managers in pivotal positions been developed based on their change capacity assessments?

3. Is the organization generally willing to use its internal resources (i.e., HR, budgeting, time allocation) to support programs such as coaching and job rotation that increase change capacity?

4. Is the organization usually willing to go outside and recruit or outsource to close the change capacity gap between the talent they need and the talent they lack?

5. Is there a cultural imperative to make the hard decisions dictated by change capacity assessments (such as removing senior people with low capacity from pivotal positions), or is the company still laboring under a culture of hope and accommodation?

For most organizations, an affirmative answer to all these questions is an ambitious goal. It's a goal, however, toward which you can move your company. Assessing and developing the change capacity of key people in your group will catalyze others in your company to do the same. Expect other managers to notice how relatively simple the process is and how extraordinary the results are. When you demonstrate that your people are well-prepared to implement just about any change strategy that comes their way, this sends a message to managers whose groups are struggling to make change happen.

You may start your company's change capacity program at an individual level, but if your company is embarking on an ambitious strategy of growth and transformation, change capacity will become everyone's business.

Notes

Preface
A Process for Making Change Happen

1. Rick Adam at Baxter International (circa 1984) was the first senior executive that I had been around to liberally use these terms to describe talent. He was Baxter's senior administrative officer at that time, with functions such as HR and succession planning reporting to him. Rick strongly advocated that for Baxter to succeed, it needed A-players, and he believed this was an issue for line management, not HR.
2. Dave Ulrich, *Human Resource Champions* (Boston: Harvard Business School Press, 1997), pp. 17–21.

Introduction
Assessing the Personal Change Capacity of Your People

1. Insight into the interplay of strategy and other factors affecting corporate performance and talent was taught at a Baxter Leadership seminar, circa 1984.
2. Robert H. Miles, *Leading Corporate Transformation: A Blueprint for Business Renewal* (San Francisco, CA: Jossey-Bass, 1997), and *Corporate Comeback: The Story of Renewal and Transformation at National Semiconductor* (San Francisco, CA: Jossey-Bass, 1997).
3. Interview with Bruce Saari, October 1990. Dr. Saari suggested that the origin of challenges and unanswered questions was at

Pepsico, although the actual source within the company was not clear. Bruce Saari was at Pepsico in the 1980s at a time when the issue of unanswered questions and challenges was used. He is a psychologist who has both solid corporate experience and has had his consulting firm for about 10 years.

4. Adapted from "Tools for Developing Successful Executives," a course developed by Michael Lombardo and Robert Eichenger circa 1990 (Greensboro, NC: Center for Creative Leadership).

5. The roadmap idea was developed in concert with Michael Cohen and the staff of the strategic planning function (Terry Westbrook, Mark Bachman, Mike Zawalski, and Barbara Allen) at Quaker Oats, Chicago, IL, circa 1994.

Chapter 1
Evaluating Five Factors

1. Mel Sorcher, *Predicting Executive Success: What It Takes to Make It into Senior Management* (New York: Wiley Press, 1985), pp. 27–53.

2. J. J. Gabarro, *The Dynamics of Taking Charge* (Boston, MA: Harvard Business School Press, 1987), pp. 71–92.

Chapter 2
Spotlighting the Two Key Measures of Change Response and Versatility

1. Concepts originated at Pepsico with Bob Eichenger and Ed Walsh, circa 1984.

Chapter 4
Identifying Group Change Capacity

1. Morgan W. McCall, et al., *The Lessons of Experience: How Successful Executives Develop on the Job* (Lexington, MA: Lexington Books, 1988).

Chapter 5
Analyzing Weak Links

1. While I'm suggesting normal psychological testing has its limitations if used clinically, I'm also recommending two instruments that are useful in bridging the gap between personality and work behaviors, and in uncovering idiosyncrasies associated with change. They are *Leadership Effectiveness Analysis* (Portland, ME: Management Research Group) and *The Occupational Personality Questionnaire* (Boston, MA: Saville and Holdsworth, Ltd.).

Chapter 7
Setting the Stage for Successful, Change-Focused Development

1. The term "culture of accommodation" is attributed to Dr. Pat Dailey, now with Lucent Technologies, who shared it in a conversation with me in 1997. I have found this description helpful in my consulting practice because it captures the essence of bureaucratic organizations that do not step up and seriously examine their talent base.
2. Permission to use the chart in Figure 7-1 comes from William Jensen of the Jensen Group. Some of the early change communications at NationsBank were influenced by these concepts. A further elaboration of these ideas will be available in the forthcoming book *Simplicity* (Cambridge, MA: Perseus Books, February 2000).
3. James L. Heskett, W. Earl Sasser, Hr., and Leonard A. Schlesinger, *The Service Profit Chain* (New York: The Free Press, 1997), pp. 10–23.

Chapter 9
Choosing the Development Options That Best Suit the Individual

1. Adapted from "Tools for Developing Successful Executives," a course developed by Michael Lombardo and Robert Eichenger circa 1990 (Greensboro, NC: Center for Creative Leadership).

2. V. J. Bentz, "Explorations of Scope and Scale: The Critical Determinant of High Level Executive Effectiveness," Technical Report No. 31 (Greensboro, NC: Center for Creative Leadership, September 1987).

3. Marvin R. Weisbord, *Productive Workplaces* (San Francisco: Jossey-Bass, 1987), pp. 154–155.

4. D. G. Bray, R. J. Campbell, and D. L. Grant, *Formative Years in Business: A Long-Term AT&T Study of Managerial Lives* (New York: John Wiley and Sons, 1974). See also Bray, D. W. and Howard, A., *The AT&T Longitudinal Studies*, pp. 266–312.

5. C. Argyris, "Teaching Smart People How to Learn," *Harvard Business Review* (May–June 1991): pp. 99–109.

6. J. Clawson, "Mentoring in Managerial Careers," in McCauley's *Work, Family, and the Career,* ed. C. B. Deer, p. 10.

7. The art and science of Individual Development Planning has been advanced by three organizations: The Center for Creative Leadership in Greensboro, NC; Personal Decisions Incorporated (PDI) in Minneapolis, MN; and Lominger, which is headed by Bob Eichenger and Mike Lombardo, located in Minneapolis, MN. Bob Eichenger and Mike Lombardo, through their product Career Architect, and Marvin Dunette, through PDI's solid work with executives, have strongly influenced much of individual development in corporate America. All three companies have specialized in this area, are considered to be state of the art in this discipline, and offer extensive, well-designed systems to write development plans.

Chapter 10
Implementing Change-Focused Coaching Techniques

1. The term "head-set" was used at Federal Express during discussions of talent to describe how individuals needed to have perspective and context, and to distinguish between attitudinal and skill set/competency issues. It was thought that individuals would be motivated if they understood more.

Chapter 11
Assessing the Organization's Capacity to Support and Facilitate Change

1. Although there are many good books on the area of organizational strategy and the implementation of strategy, I believe the best treatment and approach to the issue can be found in:

   > B. B. Tregoe, and J. W. Zimmerman, *Top Management Strategy* (New York: Simon & Schuster, 1980).
   > B. B. Tregoe, J. W. Zimmerman, R. A. Smith, and P. M. Tobia, *Vision in Action: Putting a Winning Strategy to Work* (New York: Simon & Schuster, 1989).

2. There are many variations of an organization change model; however, the consistent anchor point is the Seven-S model conceived by McKinsey. A variation of this model was developed by Bob Miles at a senior executive education conference for Quaker Oats in mid-1994. I have found in my consulting practice that a simpler version, such as the model I use in Figure 11-1, makes more sense to executives struggling with change.
3. Geary Rummler and Alan Brache, *Improving Performance: How to Manage the White Space on the Organization Chart* (San Francisco: Jossey-Bass, 1995), pp. 126–133.
4. The Organization Alignment Audit in Figure 11-2 was developed over a period of time at NationsBank, Quaker Oats, and ADT. Phil Marineau, Jim Doyle, Terry Westbrook, Paul Lucking, and Jim Shanley critiqued this tool and provided valuable insights that were used to make the instrument stronger.

Chapter 12
How Leaders at All Levels Can Make Change Happen

1. The communications work of Jim Shanley and John Harris in concert with Bill Jensen at Bank of America has been exemplary in this area, especially during the mid-1990s, when the bank was

growing at a fast pace and the issue of communications was increasingly important.

Epilogue
Change Begins One Person at a Time . . .
But It Adds Up

1. Lucent Technologies, Network Products Group, under the leadership of Dr. Pat Dailey, exemplifies the idea of HR being a true business partner. Some of the earlier writings of David Ulrich also outlined the concept and skills associated with HR becoming a "business partner." At Lucent, this concept is practiced on a daily basis.
2. In the turnaround of ADT, compensation was tailored for what the company was striving for strategically. To that end, Steve Ruzika, CEO of ADT, supplied a mantra: "Those that do . . . get. Those that don't . . . don't." It was a simple yet powerful way to be very clear about what the company's intentions were in rewarding performance.
3. The original research, called PIMS, came out of a longitudinal study begun at Harvard in 1978 that continues today. The first findings that linked talent to profitability were reported in F. W. Gluck, S. P. Kaufman, and A. S. Walleck, "Strategic Management for Competitive Advantage," *Harvard Business Review* (July–August 1980), pp. 154–161. At ADT Security Systems in 1997, we reached the same conclusions on a practical level: A-players produced at least four times the profitability as the C-players and certainly a broader spread than the D-players.
4. A. E. Pearson, "Muscle Building the Organization," *Harvard Business Review* (July–August 1987), pp. 49–55.

Further Readings

The Foundation

Most of the frameworks and models (individual change capacity and assessing organization change capability, in particular) and other views presented in this book had their origins and were tested in the early 1980s, when I was involved in large-scale change with organizations such as Federal Express, Baxter International, and NationsBank. Later versions of these ideas were tested and refined at ADT Security Services and continue in the consulting practice of Chicago Change Partners.

Various authors have, over a period of time, influenced my ideas and convictions through their professional speeches, appearances in executive education programs, articles, and personal conversations with me. Without exception, they have been gracious in mutually sharing ideas. Their books, while important and listed here for the reader's benefit, have been less influential than the personal contact I've maintained with many of them over time.

Albrecht, Karl. *The Northbound Train*. New York: AMACOM, 1994.

Beer, Michael, et al. *Managing Human Assets*. New York: The Free Press, 1984.

Clemente, Mark N., and Greenspan, David S. *Winning at Mergers and Acquisitions*. New York: John Wiley & Sons, 1998.

Egan, Gerard. *Working the Shadow Side*. San Francisco: Jossey-Bass, 1997.

Heskett, James L., Sasser, Earl, Jr., and Schlesinger, Leonard A. *The Service Profit Chain*. New York: The Free Press, 1997.

Kotter, John P. *Leading Change*. Boston: HBS Press, 1996.

McCall, Morgan W., Lombardo, Michael M., and Morrison, Ann M. *The Lessons of Experience: How Successful Executives Develop on the Job*. Lexington Books, 1988.

Miles, Robert H. *Corporate Transformation*. San Francisco: Jossey-Bass, 1997; later, *Corporate Comeback*, 1997.

Ohmae, Kenichi. *The Mind of the Strategist*. New York: Penguin Books, 1982.

Rummler, Geary, and Brache, Alan. *Improving Performance: How to Manage the White Space on the Organization Chart*. San Francisco: Jossey-Bass, 1995.

Tregoe, Benjamin B, et al. *How Top Managers Set Strategy*. New York: Simon & Schuster, 1980; and *Vision in Action*, 1989.

Ulrich, Dave, and Lake, Dale. *Organization Capability: Competing from the Inside Out*. New York: John Wiley & Sons, 1990.

Ulrich, David. *Human Resource Champions*. Boston: Harvard Business Publishers, 1997.

Whiteley, Richard C. *The Customer Driven Company*. Reading, MA: Addison-Wesley, 1991.

Index